Stories From The Big Chair

EARL MILLER

STORIES FROM THE BIG CHAIR

2009

Stories From The Big Chair

TABLE OF CONTENTS

ACKNOWLEDGEMENTS

Editing and positive thinking

I would like to give a special thanks to my friend Jeff Dennis who has made this experience yet another great adventure. Jeff wrote his first book this year and I figured who better to help me and encourage me in the process. I asked him if he would meet with me to discuss helping me edit and walk me through the do's and don'ts. It was an early morning meeting and I was feeling all energized and excited about what we were going to talk about. I told him I wanted to put a book out with my favorite stories over the last 15 years and his response was "who gives a damn?" He say's "Really who cares if you put out a book or not?" The excitement in the room came to a screeching halt and right at that moment I wondered if I had chosen the right person for the job. I had to convince him that people would enjoy the book and it was sure to be a best seller. He took the job and it has been bliss ever since. After we were done editing our friend the Spelling Bee Donna Rowles wanted to take a look at the book and only found 40 more mistakes....thanks Donna.

Artwork

I would like to thank Landon Mau for his artwork. I have always loved the art that Landon has done over the years. When it came time to think about who I would want to do the illustrations in the book I didn't have to think about it at all. I asked him to make me into a cartoon character and he said "That's easy, you are already a character!"

STORIES FROM THE BIG CHAIR

Welcome to **Stories from the Big Chair**. Hey, thanks for buying the book. If you haven't bought it and it's in your hand right now….buy it and make somebody happy…..Me…and of course you! I believe you will enjoy it. I have decided to put out this collection of stories that are some of my favorites. Let me explain a little about how this book came to be. As a regular columnist for the Weekender Magazine, each month for the last 15 years I have sat down and tried to capture something funny or important or different or crazy to give you a good laugh or cry or to be blown away about. It seems as though something always happens to me; mostly crazy things and instead of situations being a bummer I always see the humor in them. There have even been medical problems that were life threatening, but I saw only the humorous side. I think it's a lot better to laugh than to live in the negative. So, I wanted to write a book that you could pick up and read a story and get my wacky perspective on stuff……I hope you will have fun laughing at me and with me…. and enjoy my crazy life…. and always remember to enjoy each and everyday of your own.

I would like to dedicate this book to my beautiful wife Jane. She has become more beautiful each day I have been with her and more full of love minute by minute. I couldn't and wouldn't have done any of the things that have happened in the last 20 years without her smiles and love. Over the years we have had so many crazy things happen to us and have had so many great times. It has always been Earl and Jane's Excellent Adventures. To all my kids Sean, Justin, Ben, Jodie, Sheila, Rhonda and Rick I love you all so much and am blessed you all love me just the way I am. To all my Grand Children Bostin, Mika, Braden, Brody, Joel and Baby Ben…Papa loves you and is so thankful you are in my life. To my Father who I love and Mother who I miss. To Ronnie, Janice and Johnnie I love you and always remember we have each other through all the good and bad. To Steve and Diana who I love and thank for bringing me to a peaceful paradise. To all my friends who have given me the reason to enjoy each and every day here in Benicia. To June Cooper who has become my cheer leader in life and is always there to brighten up my everyday and Bob Cooper who shares with me the greatest gift of all laughter.

I thank God for each day of sobriety and giving me the gift to share it with others.

HAWAIIAN SHIRTS

This story begins in a movie theatre a bunch of years ago. I was watching a movie called Patch Adams. The character in the movie reminded me a lot of myself and how I like to take care of others and make people laugh. The movie was about half over when I noticed something and it was that when Robin Williams would come into a new scene wearing a Hawaiian shirt, it would make me smile. I started to think about it and I came up with a great idea. I was going to go home and throw all my shirts away and buy nothing but Hawaiian shirts. I thought that if seeing someone in Hawaiian shirts made me happy maybe it would do the same for other people. It would make them happy and it would give them something to talk about to break the ice to talk to me. Well, I decided to go to the mall and buy some shirts but Jane was not convinced. She told me not to throw out my shirts until I knew that was the right thing to do. She is always one step ahead of me, but this time I had a real cool feeling that this was going to be something new. So at the mall I bought three really nice Hawaiian shirts and took them home. In the morning we were headed to San Diego so my wife could meet up with her parents Bob and June. So in the morning we headed to the airport and I had my first Hawaiian shirt on and it made me feel great. Like a business man with a new suit. We stopped off at restaurant in San Jose on the way to the airport. While we were there I went to the bathroom and as I was walking out this biker about twice my size was coming towards me. I quickly moved out of his way. He looked at me and said "Hey, nice shirt" and I smiled and walked away. When I got back to my table I told my wife what just happened and she smiled and said maybe I was right. Well we got to the airport and got on the plane and while we were in the air one of the attendants came by and said "Hey nice shirt" and I was kinda blown away. We landed and headed off to the hotel to meet up with Jane's parents. When we got there we were checking in at the hotel the lady behind the counter looked up at us and smiled and said "Hey nice shirt." I was beside myself, because each time someone had said nice shirt it gave me a chance to get into a short conversation with them. In the morning June and I headed out on the train to Mexico. We ran into this young guy who mom started talking to and said he would love to guide us in Tijuana; get us around without getting messed with. So we headed into Mexico and we had a blast. Some people could have said "Hey, nice shirt," but I don't know Spanish so I would have missed it. We got back around dinner time and we headed to old town San Diego for some Mexican food. We ate at a great restaurant and while we were being seated someone had said "Nice shirt" and I told Jane's folks what was going on. After dinner we decided to go to a play that was in this real nice round theatre. The play was called "Forever Plaid" and it was about some band that was in a van heading to see the Beatles and never got there, because they crashed. The play was really fun and while it was going on I noticed one of the guys in the cast every now and then would look up our way. I thought he knew someone around us. We were about three quarters of the way up the round, kind of close to the top row. When there was about to be an intermission the guys in the play were making adjustments to the stage and the one guy who kept looking up into crowd while the play was going was now putting up some poles with strings of Christmas lights on them. I saw him look up in our direction and all of a sudden he was coming up the stairs to the top of the auditorium and he stopped at the end of our row. I was convinced he was coming up to say hello to someone sitting by us and he started excusing himself to move in front of all the people in our row. When he finally got to us he looked down at me and said "Hey man that's a real nice shirt." I was totally convinced that this was no coincidence. This was the final confirmation that I was to go home and throw all my shirts out and just buy all Hawaiian. I have since that day worn only Hawaiian shirts and have almost 250 hanging in my closet. It was true then and is still to this day; people see the Hawaiian shirt and comment. I am actually known in my town as the guy with the Hawaiian shirts. It has been a great thing for me and the best thing is that I have engaged in conversations I wouldn't have otherwise. It gives me a chance to drop seeds about my life with the full intention of helping others to enjoy each and every day.

SPELLING BEE

Here is yet another story about stuff….and this one is about my spelling, and pronunciation and grammar and as I embark on my next book I guess I will have to be a little better at my spelling. You know I have been writing these stories for15 years now and they have been good for me and I hope for you also. I have them all archived and I go back and read them from time to time and it's amazing what we have gone you through together as friends. Now you all know I have spell check, every computer has spell check, but most of the time I don't use it because I feel it takes away from my creativity….yea I know that sounds crazy, but as I sit here and pound out these words I feel like an artist and the computer screen is my canvas. This is who I am…and I really don't want to live locked up in someone else's box. It's like a brush stroke you see in a painting that you don't think belongs there….to the painter…it did, and to the buyer of the painting it did. So over the years I have gotten a lot of flack and letters about my spelling most not happy with misspelled words….. every month I usually get an email pointing out my mistakes. Probably a spelling bee winner with nothing else to do. One letter I received in the mail had all my misspelled words cut out of my story and put in an envelope and when I got the letter I opened it and they all fell out on the counter and it to me was beautiful art on my counter. One person got the words and glued them on a piece of paper kind of like a ransom note. I could tell it wasn't because it didn't make sense and I noticed all the words were misspelled. I still have it and it is also art to me. I have gotten a lot better, but the other day a co-worker was talking to me and I wouldn't mention her name, but I am going to break tradition so as to kind of thank her for her alphabetical rights.

Donna said to me, "I have to tell you when I read your stories I get so mad." She really meant it…she was getting mad while she was telling me how mad she gets. "There are always misspelled words in your stories." We didn't get into a fight…thank God…I think she could whip me…but it was a good learning experience for me. She asked me to start using spell check, because it made me look stupid with all the misspelled words. I have a feeling something in her life made spelling a pretty important feature and I totally understand it. As you know I don't misspell every word…. just some that I am either going too fast typing or that's how I hear them in my head. The one thing she did point out and I know I am guilty of it…is the misplaced to or too….well I didn't do well in high school as I was too busy building a personality. I must have missed the to-too class. So 2 help me help her not 2 get mad and you if it bothers you for this story I am going to use the number 2. It kind of adds something new 2 my stories and maybe I will think about using it in my next book. Now I'm going 2 have 2 mention her in my book for helping me with the editing. I love Donna and she has just put a new spin and a new dimension 2 the writing world. Thank you Donna and if anyone else has been having problems with my spelling I want you 2 just sit back and take a deep breath and think good thoughts. Send me some love, because I really thank you from the bottom of my heart for taking the time 2 read my stories about my crazy life for the last 15 years. Over the last 15 years we have become family. We have laughed together…cried together and I hope we have had a story 2 share with someone else. I only wish I knew as much about your lives as you know about mine. That way I could pick on you for things you do that are different than I do them. I have put my life out there for you 2 have fun with and I hope I can continue 2 be a part of your lives. I would love 2 think that when I'm gone…. I will be remembered as that wild, crazy, weird, funny, unique, larger than life, caring, loving, big strange loveable dork . Excuse me for my faults, as I look upon them as laughable art.

TOOL TIME EARL

J ane and I have just purchased our first home together (Condo) or as some people have let me know—Town home—I prefer Condo it sounds more like a home than an apartment—which is really what it is—an apartment they call a condo to sell for more money, because who would buy an apartment? Well first off—I must say something about the price of homes, and condos in our quaint little town of Benicia -GIVE ME A BREAK! You would think that after someone has lived in your new place (their old place) for 25 years the price would go down not up. Now let me tell you what we are doing to our new Condo—GUTTING IT! Nothing is the way we want it, well let me rephrase that—nothing is the way my wife wants it...I believe we were looking for the designer showcase...so we got out the sledge hammer, our new power drill, a new sander, putty knives, jack hammer, crow bars, (stud finders.. my wife's idea) and screw drivers and completely demolished the inside of our new place. It just so happens that the owners dropped by the day after we completely GUTTED the kitchen, and they looked a little confused, and upset and scared, because as I found out later as of this time we hadn't qualified for our loan yet, and as their lips trembled they asked if we knew when the escrow was going to close, and I said I hoped we were going to qualify for the loan. They walked out of the condo looking very confused, but I could see that in their hearts they were at peace that we had done an excellent job destroying their condo. Now starts the rebuilding work—first it's remove all the wallpaper from all the walls to get ready to paint—I jump at the chance to start fixing up my new place (Never did the wallpaper thing before) and volunteer to strip the wallpaper—I figure it will probably take me about 2 or 3 hours, and it's on to my next project—WRONG—3 days later, and 3 layers later I'm closing in on bare sheetrock—back hurts, arms hurt, legs hurt, hands are all cut up from being a dork...If you ever get the chance to strip wallpaper—don't!! I'm not really that well versed in electricity either, and the funniest thing happened when I was washing down the walls with TSP while standing on cement— holding on to the edge of the wall with the metal strip on the corner edge—I felt this weird tingling pain go down my arm and through my body ..I thought it was my shingles (yes I have shingles again) so I tried it again to see if I would get the same sensation, or was it my shingles.... DUUUUUUHHHHHHHHHHHH.. I was getting electrocuted—I learned a good, and may I say.... very educated lesson. As we speak I'm heading over to primer (which I thought they only did to cars) the entire condo, and I'll report back in just a few hours. Ok I'm back—no not a few hours—2 days later. Arms hurt, neck hurts, legs hurt, back hurts, eyes hurt—you ask why do my eyes hurt? You look up at a ceiling all day and roll paint, and you will understand. Oh and I got my first experience at oil base paint in a closed room—Flashback to the 60's—kinda like a "smoking the banana peel" headache. Ever heard someone in the construction trade tell you "a couple of hours and we'll be all done!" Well I think next time I will ask to pay for the hours they think it will take, and not what it really takes (great idea). Well it looks like this is going to be an on-going adventure, as this weekend we are jack hammering out tile -(big thick tile) they call Mexican pavers, and painting the entire condo. I will let you know what kind of fun I had working my little fingers to the bone. Now I'm kind of getting the idea of why they charge more for a home when it gets old, because you have to do so much to keep it looking young like us!

HERE'S LOOKIN AT YA

We'll there is a lot going on as far as adventures go, but I thought I would fill you in on a freaky thing that happened to me on the way to the grocery store. I was going shopping at Raley's one day about a month ago, and stopped in to see my eye doctor, and he asked about the 3 lbs of skin hanging over my eyes being held up by my eyelashes and clothespins. He suggested that I have the skin removed, and donate it to a skin graft clinic in case someone needed a complete body makeover. Yea that's a lot of skin, and now you know why I haven't waved to you when you drove by. I couldn't see you!! Ok I set up the appointment to have the operation done, and they promised me I would look 10 years younger, and a lot like Tom Cruise. So I go into the hospital (Queen of the Valley) I know what you're thinking….. but NO. The hospital is located in Napa, and is a great hospital….I went there some years ago when all the bees in Napa decided to have lunch…. and the menu was my face. I came very close to my final exit, but I lived. (Now my wife calls me Honey) So on with the story….on my way to the hospital I thought to myself…Self…what the heck am I doing? Maybe the skin is there to protect my eyes from the UV rays from the sun or maybe I'm not supposed to see the whole picture or something like that, and I'm going to have it hacked off. Well I checked into the hospital, and lost the "scared out of my skin feeling" and settled down. I was thinking ahead before I got to the hospital…I put on a pair of Joe Boxer flannel shorts, and I sure am glad I did. The little apron they gave me to cover up had no back—you know what I'm talking about…so I was glad to have a little covering. Jumped into a rolling hospital bed—flipped on the TV…dialed up a golf tournament and it was Tiger Woods and I for the next two hours. A nurse comes to get me, and wheels me off to the operating room. The guy who is suppose to put me under isn't there yet so the doctor starts to draw on my eyelids with a magic marker....kind of scary...I ask (very concerned) is the anesthesiologist going to be here soon? I see him walk in and two seconds later I'm having an out of body experience. The doctor asks me to open my eyes and look at her finger. I open my eyes, and I'm kinda wondering where am I? The drugs they gave me made it real easy to allow the doctor to clip away without me flinching once. I could hear the skin being cut, and watched them working, but I was out of it enough and didn't know it was me they were working on. The next thing I realize is I'm in my bed again with the TV on waiting for the nurse to come get me to have the operation....if it wasn't for the bandages on my eyes I probably wouldn't have known I had the operation. The operation was a HUGE success—the skin was donated to Animal Kingdom, and an elephant was gifted with a total skin graft—I was glad I could help. I look like I was mugged, and have hopes that the look of me wearing eye liner goes away soon, or I will be the Queen of the Valley...I just hope they didn't cut off to much skin, so I can shut my eyes to sleep. I'll keep an eye open for ya!!

PULLING TEETH

This has been a pretty busy month, but I'm sorry to say not a REAL exciting one—well except maybe the guy in the restaurant up in Kelseyville CA. Yea….Jane and I took a ride up to what we believe will be our retirement area when we either win the lottery, or someone ends up loving us so much they leave us all their money. (I guess we will be retiring in Benicia.) Let's get back to the Grill in Kelseyville…what a great place to eat…little town…little restaurant…little money…everything on the menu is… how can I say…(cheap) like it is suppose to be. Well the fun started when a table filled up at the front of the restaurant, (remember.. small restaurant) and this family sits down, and all of a sudden it seemed like someone was either very hard of hearing, or completely deaf—because the gentleman of the table which appeared to be the father was talking—well actually—he was yelling his conversation at the people at his table like he had headphones on and couldn't hear himself and was listening to AC-DC full blast. Instead of letting it bother us we just kicked back enjoyed our meal, and took in the small town atmosphere. We did get the scoop (couldn't help from ease dropping) on everything that was happening in his life, and anyone that had come in contact with him for the last 20 years. It kind of reminded me of something you would have seen in the movie Deliverance…although nobody else seemed to mind…except for the guy from the local phone Co. sitting in the booth next to us, but he cleared it up for us…he said the guy was the local dentist, and it seems as though it was his day off, and he had been out drinking most of the night before, and maybe all morning. "OH that small town feeling" We are really looking forward to settling down in a nice quiet little town like Kelseyville!! Our suggestion to anyone traveling or moving to this small little town up in the lakes area.... Choose your dentist carefully!! And maybe invest in some earplugs. I do have to say besides the screaming dentist...the restaurant was great, and everybody made you feel like you were family.

CABO SHINGLES

Headed down to Cabo San Lucas to relax and OHHHHHHHHHH did we have a blast! It was a vacation that was badly needed. I had just had my eye operation to take the skin away from my eyes so I could see again, and just to add to the drama I got a real bad case of shingles right after the operation. I thought the eye operation hurt until I was lucky enough to get shingles. Where did this disease come from anyway? Chicken Pox that sits inside your body until it feels like your immune system is at an all time low—then it attacks! -It attacks big time! Feels kinda like an electric shock to an open wound to certain areas of your body at any given moment, hurts, itches, ouch, ouch, ouch and all around just feels BAD! I've known some people who have had shingles, and I always thought what's the big deal? The big deal is…this disease sits around in your body for 30 or 40 or 50 years waiting to attack at just the right moment, and when it does it's something only those who have had it understand. Some people say it comes from being stressed out, and I kind of believe that cause some people tell me I'm a stress case.

50 OR TWO THIRDS

Yea it's finally happened—Big Old Earl has turned the corner on the aging scene. Now I look at things a lot different— first instead of calling myself 50 I'm going to use the term two thirds or as some of my friends would remind me—nine tenths. I'm telling you though I don't feel a day over 49, and mentally I still feel 25. So what's the big deal about turning 50? I feel so fortunate to be 50—ya know we aren't guaranteed any, and to get to 50 with the kind of life I've lived is an absolute miracle. Now what are the benefits of turning 50?—well I just found out that my working at the grocery store for about 8 years when I was just a punk has paid off When I left the retail clerks union years ago...and I do mean years ago.....I went down and they gave me a withdrawal card...this card stayed in my wallet for the last 25 years and it was tattered.....I had jumped in lakes, pools, the ocean and forgot to take my wallet out of my pocket, so what I ended up with looked like a piece of old crumbled up toilet paper with numbers on it......I had even lost my wallet quite a few times over the years, but always seemed to find It sooner or later.....I was curious to see if I had anything coming.... knowing very well I didn't work long enough, but a friend of mine I ran into at a grocery store told me that if we got a withdrawal card when we quit we could get back to work and make up the time to get to 10 years vested. I called the Retail Clerks Union, and thought if I had to I could work a couple of years as a courtesy clerk up here at my local Safeway. To vest my 10 years I would do it. The lady from the local union on the phone told me to come on down and we could talk. I was pretty excited and not only because it was my birthday, but that I might get to bag groceries at Safeway. I got to the Union offices and went inside and talked to a lady and she said let's go in to my office so I can bring this up on the computer. I explained that I thought I only had about eight and a half years before I quit. She started looking up my withdrawal number and looked up at me with a big smile on her face and said I was vested and I could start collecting in less than 2 weeks if I wanted too or I could wait until I was 55 and get $300.00 or wait until I turned 62 and it would go to about $500.00 and I stopped her right there and said I need to get it right now. I am really not sure I am going to be around that much longer….. so—YAHOOOOOOO! I did one thing right when I was young, in spite of myself! Now I'm retired as of June 1st, 2000 with $128.29 a month. See ya on the golf course, and at the beach! Retirement—Ahhhhhh the good life.

WE KNOW RENO

Last month we went on a four day trek which included Benicia to Reno and then on to Las Vegas. Let's start with Reno....I have been seeing these beautiful billboard signs along all the freeways in the Bay Area advertising the newest addition to the casinos to Reno..This marketing company ought to win some advertising awards, because every time I would drive by a billboard I wanted to keep driving and head up to my luxury hotel room.....It's a beautiful picture of a fabulous casino and with a beautiful river just outside your window, spa, pool and everything you would expect from a world class casino...in Reno! OK I was fooled one more time...I just wanted to stay for one night and tried to just get one night, but they said the rooms were all booked up unless you stayed two nights....I think the same guy who designed the billboards answered the phone...so I booked the room.....we headed up to Reno and on the drive up I had daydreams about laying in my lounge chair watching beautiful people stroll by right after my nice swim in the pool and then a pampering massage at the spa. When we got there I didn't see that many cars or people for that matter. Remember when they told me on the phone the place was booked well nobody showed up, or they showed up and heard what I was about to hear and left. While checking in we were informed that the pool and spa wouldn't be built for months. Now my attitude was getting a little out of control, as I realized my dreams had been shattered...I came to lay by the pool and relax in the sun and let all my troubles float away. To say the least I was bummed, but my wife said hey we'll have a blast no matter what, so I chilled. I got our room key and headed up the elevator to our room...Our tiny room...I have been in walk-in closets bigger than this room and upon opening the drapes I noticed that even though the drapes were open there was no light coming in the room, none at all…. Why, because the beautiful **dome room bar** downstairs was just outside my window blocking my beautiful view and the sun. At this point I wouldn't have wanted to be the check-in clerk. I went back downstairs and was now way beyond a bad attitude, but I was maintaining…the person at the check in desk must have also been the bell clerk and the cook and the maid and the store clerk, so it took awhile to get some attention. Finally when I had explained how I wasn't told about the pool or the spa not being finished or the dome outside my window and the only way to stay was to book two nights I was upset and the fact that they had booked the room that had the dome outside the window and they knew that I wanted some answers. The desk clerk wasn't that together maybe a French fry short of a happy meal at best. She told me that they were going to help me out and change my room and send me up five floors…just above the dome. The bathroom was so small that if you wanted two people in it one would have to stand on the vanity….forget it!! I really had a rough time that weekend but I stayed out of the hotel and casino until I had to go to sleep each night. What comes to mind is those famous words of the Who…….We won't get fooled again!

FLOWING WATER

OK let's go to Vegas baby...........You know the one thing you can say about Vegas.........BIG, BIG, BIG, BIG...BIG rooms, BIG bathrooms, BIG buildings, BIG money....and don't forget BIG breasts. Got a real good deal on a 3 night stay at the Aladdin which had recently been rebuilt. It was clear that everybody had got a good deal on their rooms. The casino had a special to get people in for the new opening. I was in the lobby for check in...with about a half a million people and an hour in the line, but we met some nice folks from around the country and really didn't mind...cause I love Vegas...I don't drink, and I really don't gamble much...Got up to my room and WOW...This isn't Reno Baby.....just outside my window...the Beautiful Bellagio with their water show, Paris and the tower right next door, and a view of all the casinos...I love this place. When you walk into the room there are these big bottles of bottled water in a real pretty blue bottle, and I took my bottle and drank it down, and went out and when I came back to my room there was another one. So I took it and drank it down...left and upon entering my room I noticed another one had appeared...I went to the pool and forgot my water so I went to buy one, and they were five bucks...and I thought wow I should have brought down a free one....when I came back to my room....another one was waiting for me...I felt like I was more than getting my money's worth of the room just by the free water.... They must have a buzzer that rings somewhere when you lift the bottle, because they are right there with a new one...this went on for two days until I picked up one of my bottles and finally read the little paper thing around my bottles neck.....These bottles of water are FIVE BUCKS and we will be checking your room to make sure you always have fresh water!!!! About $40 bucks worth of water later...I finally got the picture...nothings free except the air and the sun..and I think that somehow they are charging for those without me knowing about it. We had a blast and would highly recommend Vegas to everyone...except compulsive gamblers, sex addicts or alcoholics.

WANNA BUY A ROLEX?

J ane and I headed off to Vegas for some over 100 degree temperatures that we have been waiting for in the Bay Area, but haven't seen as of yet. We stayed at the new Mandalay Bay Hotel, and I've got to tell ya—what a nice, big, fun, and beautiful hotel. This place has 3,300 rooms which would accommodate just about everyone in Benicia. Along with the 3,300 rooms comes a worker for every room. I asked how many employees, and they told me 3,000. Now let's do some figuring—3,000 x at least 10 dollars x 40 hours a week that's one million two hundred thousand just for the regular workers per week. Now throw in all the executives and all the staff to keep them working, and the lawyers, and all their lunch and dinner comps. Now all the electricity, and the water bill, and the money it took to build it which was somewhere around 900 million, and throw in a few extras like insurance, and retirement funds, and handi-wipes for those of us who spend 100 dollars in nickels to make sure this place stays in business. I would hate to see this place fold up. So please if you go down to Vegas—first tell them I sent you, and then spend at least 100 dollars—they need to pay some bills. Now let me tell you about the hotel—they have an 11 acre pool area with a sandy beach that seats at least 1,000 on the beach in lounge chairs—yea I said beach. There is a wave machine that produces 5 foot waves for body surfing. I body surfed quite a bit while I was there and one of the neat things is there are so many people body surfing, as you catch the wave you just grab a kid and use them as a boogey board. There is nothing like sitting at the ocean in Vegas. They also have what they call the lazy river....you jump in and just float around and around without exerting any energy, as you go around the river there are waterfalls you go through to

keep you cool….Watch your stuff though—I lost my gold watch….
someone was obviously watching me while I was getting ready to go
in the water. I probably look like a Rolex man, and you know I feel
like one, but I'm not! When I came back after an hour in the lazy
river my watch had been stolen from my pocket of my shirt I left
on my chair. I guess someone probably needed to know what time
it was. Thank God it was my Seiko with the broken lens, and the
goofy band. I'm sure when they went to pawn it they probably got
laughed at and got paid a roll of nickels, but maybe they struck it
rich with the nickels, or just got a free handi-wipe.

2 SURF OR NOT 2 SURF

I am kind of off track this week....I haven't lost anything except my keys a few times this month. My wife tells me that we are going on this cabbage vegetable soup diet. She says that you lose about a pound a day....No kidding....you just eat a head of cabbage a day and I guarantee you will lose a pound a day...and a lot of friends. I'm going to try it, because I'm stupid that way....I've tried everything else why not the cabbage diet? Now that the summer has passed me by and my Speedos are still in the dresser I really am concerned about next summer...I have given a lot of thought to my surfing career and have come to the conclusion that I might just be getting a bit old and big for competition.....I went to Mexico a few weeks ago and jumped out into the surf to do some body surfing and the waves were pretty rough and the rip tide was moving pretty strong...I went straight out and in about 3 or 4 minutes I was a few hundred yards down the coast. It took everything I had to get back in after catching a few waves. When I finally reached the sand where I could stand I was beaten down by the crashing waves. I have a small part of me that thinks this could be for younger folks. I am still going to try, but the desire is starting to kind of go away..... Maybe I will just take pictures....You know I was in Vegas and went to Mandalay Bay and they have a wave machine and a nice beach with beautiful girls with hard bodies just walking around for your eyes and waiters on the beach......I had a blast catching the waves there....... and body surfing along with 500 other kids and moms. I think I will give the surfing thing a few more tries and then I will make up my mind...maybe volleyball or frisbee or just sun tanning would be a lot better on my body....Probably not...C-ya next month.

FIVE BRIDGE TOUR

We had a visitor from Dallas, Texas (no not George Bush) who had never been here before and we wanted to take him sight seeing around the Bay Area. One morning I decided what better way to see the Bay Area than to do the five (5) bridge tour. Now I know what you are thinking.... did I miss that concert? Well the five (5) bridge tour starts in Benicia...over the (#1) Benicia Bridge...through Martinez, Concord, Pleasant Hill, Walnut Creek, Lafayette, Orinda, Berkeley, Oakland, and over the (#2) Bay Bridge through San Francisco....trying to get to the Golden Gate Bridge took a while.....a long while...We wanted to let him see some sights so we stopped off at Pier 39...**it was a holiday**...I have never seen this many people in one place at one time. You would think they were giving away free fruit at the fruit stand at the pier... Have you ever bought fruit from the fruit stand on Pier 39? Did you use your Gold Card? Or maybe gave them one of your children? A few large strawberries and a pear.....runs about 10 bucks...you got to be kidding me...If that's what it cost to stay healthy...give me a corn dog, and an ice cream in a chocolate waffle cone. While at Pier 39 our friend was really excited when he heard the sound of those big old sleepy seals that have taken over the marina dock space next to the pier. Now I'm no financial wizard but what do you think the guy or company that was renting out the most prime location in S.F. thinks about the newest addition (sea lions) to the tourist attractions of Pier 39? I just bet they were trying everything possible to get rid of the seals and some animal loving person thought "we will fight to keep the seals happy" and give them a place to sleep. Well it's off to the Golden Gate...I have a little trouble navigating my way through the City...and this day was just a bit troubling...I couldn't find anything…I was looking for the Golden Gate Park, because I know the bridge is at one end of the park, but Where's the Park? Drove up one way and down the next. Finally driving over the top of a really steep street I noticed an area with a lot of trees…I started driving towards it I noticed a lot of others were heading my way…this was a weekend when there was a Wine and Cheese and Music Festival…..great time to be stuck in traffic. I'm just looking for the biggest structure in S.F. and I can't find it…Ah Haa…I run into traffic backed up for what seems to be a mile or two heading in the right direction. I get real excited knowing I'm near. We sit in the traffic for quite a while and get to move up one car length at a time….YES.. YES..there in the distance is the Gold I have been looking for……a while later…THE BRIDGE…over the (#3) Golden Gate.. Through Sausalito, Marin, and now we are heading to the Richmond Bridge when our guest notices one of our more famous attractions….San Quentin…he is so excited he can't contain himself, so we pull off the road and head up to the main gate. We get out and have him stand in front of the BIG sign to take a picture to show his parents…. San Quentin State Prison…he seems way more excited about this historical landmark than the seals or the fruit at the pier. We chat with the guard at the gate….who is there to make sure no one breaks in!! I guess the guard noticed our guest was young and pretty excited about being at San Quentin…So he starts telling him what kind of mean and nasty people live inside…and tells him he better think twice about what kind of things he does that could be against the law…..just to scare him a bit…I wonder how the guard thought to say something, because boy I didn't say anything, but the reason the visitor was with us was to dry out from heroin and clean up some of his past. We take off and it's over the (#4) Richmond San Rafael Bridge….through Point Richmond, Richmond, Pinole, Hercules, Crockett..and then over the (#5) Carquinez Bridge…YES it's finally…Bridge Number 5…through Vallejo, Glen Cove and back to beautiful Benicia. What a day…I have a suggestion if you have guests…forget the 5 bridge tour and take them to the movies at the mall and maybe out to dinner, or better yet rent them a car…

buy them a map...and let them go by themselves....it could be a heck of a lot cheaper...especially if they love fruit. If you do decide to make the 5 bridge tour...pack yourself a nice lunch...with extra fruit...maybe you can sell some at the pier. The bridge toll is only 4 bucks at the Bay Bridge and 4 bucks at the Carquinez. Now if you eat lunch inside the car...the whole vacation day will cost you EIGHT BUCKS...you can't beat it!! A word of advice is: don't go on a holiday...any holiday....

WHO'S RUNNING?

Remember me telling you I passed the dreaded Real Estate Exam? Well do you remember what month I passed......August...that's right August...well I just got my license in the mail on the 16th of November. Seems as the State Department had to get together with the FBI and the DEA and the CIA and the local police and decide if I had paid my debt to society for getting arrested for some weed in 1968 which was 33 years ago. I don't know if you've seen my advertising signs, but I put up some signs all around town and on my Jeep and a few other vehicles. The signs say **Earl Miller for Realtor....**I was trying to get them out before the election...because I thought it would be kind of funny.....I bought them a couple of months ago and had them sitting waiting for the license. I don't know if it would have been more effective before the election or now, but I have gotten quite a wide range of peoples thoughts about the signs and I would like to share a few with you.....One very nice lady asked me if I was the only person running, because she hadn't seen any other signs of other candidates running...Another nice person commented who seemed very concerned "I didn't know you had to run to be a realtor"....And yet another said "wow I heard the test to be a realtor was really hard to pass and now you also have to be elected?"...OK just one more.........."When is the election?" I didn't really expect all the different thoughts, but it has been quite amusing and if you haven't voted yet.......please keep me in mind on election day!!

ALL THAT JAZZ

Another Concert story—yea I know, but this one is Jazz and I know you're gonna love the ending—unlike some of the endings in the past. OK every now and then we get invited to some pretty neat stuff. I don't know if the people really like us, or they just know that I'm gonna mention their names. The concert is the world renowned Paolo Conte from Italy, and I have never heard of him, so I ask my friend Peppino D'Agostino, who is from Italy, and not in the mafia….and he tells me I shouldn't miss this. He says this guy is a big hero like maybe Dylan, or the Beatles is to us. The folks who invited us are nice enough to let me bring another couple. Do you know how hard it is to find someone to go to a Jazz concert? Usually if they have heard of the person it's still hard, but if they haven't.. they make up excuses like—We are dog sitting and can't get out, but I wish we could spare the time. So we went through our list of friends…all two of them and the first couple said OK if I would drive, pay bridge toll, parking and buy them dinner. Well I thought it would be a stress free evening for me so it was a date. The neat thing about the evening was we were invited to the pre-show…to meet the star and mingle while eating fine foods. So the pre-show started at 6:00 pm and we thought we would show up fashionably late so we left the house at 6:00 pm to arrive a little after 7:00. Well it's not too often we head to the City on a Friday night…and it's not too often we go out when it is raining so hard the windshield wipers hardly work, but we are troupers. Got on highway I-80 and got to Richmond and the traffic was bumper to bumper all the way to the Bay Bridge, and then into the City. Now it is around 8:30pm and remember I'm not supposed to stress about anything, so I remain very cool about the two and a half hour drive—and knowing we have preferred parking we can just pull up and get right in to the concert—NOT—we drive up to the parking garage and the attendant say's there is not even one spot available. So we drive around for about 15 minutes and figure we better let the girls out and we can go find a spot a little further away from the concert. Well we did and then drove up and down every street within a mile and the only parking available was in a red zone. Now it's coming up on 9:00pm and there is a sense of gloom that has set in with Phil and I. So we head down one of the City's steepest streets and within about a little over a half mile straight down we find a parking garage. Now we're happy for a few minutes until we realize we are going to have to walk up the steepest hill in San Francisco, in the pouring rain, to see someone we hope will still be on stage when we get there. I don't know if I mentioned it but I was wearing a suit—yea a suit—I don't ever wear a suit. Well up the hill we go laughing all the way—what else could we do? Every few minutes Phil asks if I'm ok—I guess he notices me holding on to my heart and breathing like it could be my last breath of air. Well we made it...and off into the building...wet, late, exhausted and a little stressed out. We get into the building and this is one of those concerts where you can't go in while the performer is performing. Now it is time to go in and we spot our dry comfortable wives and friends. The band starts up plays one song and then intermission. We stand around and talk about how good the band is and then back in for the last of the concert. We get to hear 6 songs and then—yea you guessed it...a fun walk back down to the car. You are probably asking—what about a taxi—well we were asking the same thing ourselves. There were none, so we headed down the hill...we could have rolled down, but knew we would have picked up enough speed to kill a pedestrian, so we walked.

OH what a night!

SURFS UP DUDE

Let's get right to the part of old age…I just turned 51 and as I look back the only thing I can relate this too is when my father was 51 and I was 25, I thought my dad was old. I don't mean real old…just old…like not cool old. Well now that I'm 51 I have a better perspective on it…I'm cool….well at least I think I am, or maybe I'm just kidding myself. I dress like a 25 year old…and maybe I should think about that too…..OK now it's off to Santa Cruz for the weekend with full intentions of making a comeback of the 60's. When I was young I used to make it to the beaches quite frequently with a few friends. I bought my first surfboard (longboard) from a place like the Home Depot called CBS Hardware in Concord. We would cut school quite often and head down to the beaches. I never was any good as a surfer, but if you were to ask me to this day I would tell you a whole different story. I thought I was the Duke Kahanamoku of Santa Cruz. I don't know if you remember the wind surfing story of two years ago, but it was kind of like that. I think I spent more time thinking and talking about me being a surfer than I ever participated as one. I guess I really wanted the attention that was going on about being "COOL" as a surfer. Talk about a quick change in who I was, I remember being a "greaser" with Dixie peach in my hair and a fine torch with a little peroxide in it and I actually thought I was Bad! Walking around school one day (acting bad) I remember seeing a guy wearing white with blue pinstripe slacks with cuffs and he had a really cool hair-do…blonde and parted down the middle and everyone was all over him—Yes this was our first glimpse at a LA surfer. It only took about a week for my torch to be combed to the side…total removal of the Dixie peach and my hair split down the middle and you guessed it.. I was now a surfer! Hadn't seen the water yet, but wore the clothes—talked the talk—bought the records and played the part. Now about 35 years later...I decided that at 51 it was time to reclaim my title (in my head) as Mr. Santa Cruz. We booked a room at the Dream Inn on the beach and I stood on the balcony and dreamed of being number one. I told Jane I was going out the next morning and "Shoot the Curl" "Hang Ten" baby...it was Cowabunga time for pops. She freaked out and said "no way dude" and tried to explain to me the downfalls of all my physical conditions mixed with the pounding surf. Well as stubborn as I am I refused to accept the 51 and done theory. So the next morning I was up early...took a walk to "Steamers Lane" got all worked up and went back to the Hotel. Explained to Jane it "was something I just had to do" so I waited for the waves to pick up to go out. Well the weather was a blistering 85 degrees and the water was like glass. The previous day there were about 300 surfers out in this area with nice waves all day and today "my big comeback day" there was one guy who just sat and looked out into the ocean waiting for the perfect wave all day. Maybe the Surf God's were with me and maybe my wife was right...but I will forever (in my own mind) be the "cool old guy" who could have made the greatest comeback in surfing history and been the "surfing champion of the world" if I could have just had another chance. Surfs up Dudes! & Dudettes!

MONEY, IT'S A HIT!

I gotta tell you that last month I bought stock and 3 hours later the company went broke...yup bankrupt. I thought maybe some good fortune would soon come my way. Oh was I mistaken...I was going to show a home over in Vallejo and my head was full of dreams of becoming the number one Real Estate Agent in all of California. As I was turning the corner onto the street the home was on....all of a sudden BAM..I was being moved sideways by an oncoming vehicle...A construction truck...Did I mention I was in my wife's Volvo that I only get to drive on special occasions. When my car finally stopped I got out and went to talk to the nice gentleman who had just pulled out from the curb and smashed into me. I walked over to his vehicle and a car stops in front of the construction truck and the man from the car got out and was screaming at the guy for being in the middle of the road. The guy who hit me starts yelling back at the man and all of a sudden it seems like they are going to start throwing blows....It got really crazy for a moment there. The guy jumps back in his car and takes off...A cop shows up and everything seems cool and he writes a report. I know from the bottom of my heart that nobody was coming down Tennessee when I was turning left, and the guy in the truck was pulling away from the curb. So I left thinking no problem...I live in a world where everyone is honest....<u>NOT</u>...my insurance company calls me and tells me the guy has filed a claim against my insurance company for damages...funny thing...When the cop was looking over both our vehicles the owner of the truck says "Wow look nothing happened to my truck at all...not even a dent" I sure mashed that Volvo".... I can't believe it, but I should have known...well we rent a car which at the time we know is covered by the other insurance company, because we know it was his fault. My wife was driving the rental car a few days after we dropped off the Volvo…(which had a $500 deductible) She runs the rental into a post in a parking lot and rips some paint off the bumper…we call the insurance company…guess what…$500 deductible. Now we have no cars and I am driving my dependable Jeep home when all of a sudden under the hood it sounds like two cars just collided. Yes you guessed it….now we have 3 cars in the shop. My insurance company forgot to ask me over the last 10 years when I got coverage if I wanted to be fully covered for a rental car if I ever had an accident and the bill for the 20 days for the car was a whopping $708.00. Before I was leaving the parking lot of the rent- a-car place…I made a special call to the insurance company and asked if I was fully covered…she happily said YES…Didn't mention if I got into a little fender bender I would have to come up with another $500. I'm not a happy camper. I want a reenactment of the accident and I want everyone in court. I realize now that if I would have sold the house I was going to…at least I would have broken even. As the next week approached I was really in a great mood….what can ya do? Things happen and these things were only material things…nobody, or no-thing was hurt…except my bank account..my nerves..my belief in the system..my understanding of the truth…and last but not least my belief in the insurance industry..Now I haven't heard back from the insurance company yet on the final outcome, but I will tell you this…next month I will be letting you know if I am still with the same company. Just when I thought it was over for the disasters a few days later I get a call from my daughter….I'm out at a restaurant (Randy's)…just ordered…and she says "Your house is an inch and a half deep under water and it's a mess". I can't take another disaster…so I tell her I'll be up to the house after lunch. I get home and yes it's a mess, everything is wet; the rugs are soaked, the carpet is like a slip and slide. Thank God my daughter's boyfriend (Rick) was with her…he cleaned up everything before I could get home…what a guy…Then the carpet cleaners come up to the house, hooks up a dryer for the next 24 hours and saved the carpet.

Following month....... Ok let's get started on the insurance and car episode...Well it turned out just the way I thought it would..."nobody wants to work for their money anymore." You know I didn't get to meet the adjuster who sat at her desk and made the decision to call it my fault without really doing any investigating. I wonder if maybe it was a bad day, or maybe she had someone pick on her in High School with the name Earl.....ya never know, but I do know this.....the accident was not my fault!..and it did cost me almost $1,600 out of my pocket. I asked them to get in touch with the cop who kinda witnessed the accident to ask him if he remembered the guy saying "No damage to my truck", but NO I guess they were busy. I did get asked to investigate it and to go take pictures myself, by someone who I send money to each month, but I was kinda under the impression that was their job. Maybe all the insurance folks at my agents office that day were trying to decide if the rates should go up, or maybe it was around lunchtime and they were trying to decide on pizza or a burrito. Does it sound like I'm a little bit bitter?.....I am....they sent me a letter saying I could fight it if I wanted to.....Maybe they would like to go to work for me and then I could find the time.....enough of that......Call me stupid, but I am with the same company...Yea CALL ME STUPID! I wonder if the guy who hit me will all of a sudden come up with a whip lash, or broken back, or maybe something just to get a few weeks off from work and a few extra bucks from me.

DUMPSTER DIVING

Ever been right, and someone just doesn't think so? Well the other day I went over to the Meyer's Cookware warehouse in Vallejo—**big sale!** I was amazed at the big discounts for what I believe is the best cookware available. OK here it is…I shop around the store until I find the set I want, and it's regularly priced at $550.00 now on sale for $149.00 I can't believe my eyes, so I go up front and the girl at the counter hands me a coupon for another 30% off, now I really can't believe it. Total of the bill is $112.65 for a 10 piece cookware set. Now on the way out I also get a free gift…I already feel like I've gotten a free gift. Well the next day comes, and I've told everyone in town about the **BIG SALE**, and my wife and I head back over to the place to purchase something for a gift exchange for a party we will be attending. I hope you saw the (we) in the above sentence—yea—Jane and I are now shopping for a gift that is suppose to cost about $10 but we feel like making it something special, and we figure if we spend about $20 it will be really about $50 in value, and that will make someone pretty happy. We find a gift to give at the party, and we continue to walk around the store. Well Jane sees stuff (she needs) and by the time we get around the last corner we have **(SAVED)** hundreds of dollars—just coming to buy a $20 gift we saved hundreds of dollars. Now we did have to spend $300.00 to save all that money, but somehow we saved! Coming around the last corner we come to the set I bought yesterday—**AH HAA**—marked down to $129.00 today, and just yesterday $149.00. I feel a little hurt. When I'm at the register I ask for the manager, and she explains that it couldn't have been $149.00 yesterday, because she had changed the price before I came in—well I know how much I paid because I told half of Benicia. She tells me to bring in my receipt, and she will credit me back. We'll I am a freak when it comes to receipts, and I keep them all for at least 2 years...just in case. So I go home to get my receipt, and guess what? I can't find it anywhere...now I have to let you know I don't really care about the $20, because I know if we go back it will cost me hundreds just to get my $20. But I do have to prove that I am not wrong, so I start looking all over the house, and my car, and Jane's car, and yes...I go to the dumpster yes the dumpster, because I had taken out the garbage the day before. Climbing in the dumpster is not something I am proud of, but I have to prove I'm right so I find my bag of trash, and I start to go through it piece by piece. I can't believe I didn't put my receipt where I put every receipt I have ever had! Running my hands through the garbage is making me sick, and mad. Just as I am half way into the bags a couple of neighbor women walk up, and oh-boy am I embarrassed. I'm new in the neighborhood, and I'm elbow deep into a bag of garbage that they have no idea why. They keep talking, and I wait for a chance to tell them exactly what I'm doing, but they keep talking—I finally have to break into the conversation, because I'm feeling really stupid at this point. I explain about the pots, and pans thing, and they just look at me like (yeah sure). Well after all the embarrassment, and the humiliation...**NO RECEIPT.** I can't believe that I'm not going to be able to prove I'm right! So back into the house, and guess what? Yup I go through my pile of receipts for the last time and in my pile of receipts the very bottom one is the one I'm looking for. I was right and it was $149.00 the day before. I am so excited and I smell like a dumpster of garbage, but I'm off to the warehouse to prove I'm right. (what is my problem?) The manager is very very nice...and she refunds my money. It was probably because she wanted me out of the store, because people were complaining about the smell.....I get my $20 back but end up spending another $100. I could have left well enough alone, and saved $80 if I would not have had to prove I was right—**NO NOT ME!**

LOVING THE DEPOT

Oh-Boy do I have a few things to tell you about what I have learned about a remodel—probably everybody out there knows—but for those who don't...listen up! First we'll start with painting—seems easy—just move the paintbrush up and down until the wall is painted. Well how about cut in the edges, and what about the baseboard, and what about the trim, and what about the second coat, and what kind of brush, and flat, satin, or gloss, and what about the difference between primers, and oil base (and speaking about oil base)- I went in to a store, and asked for some oil base paint—a very well known store at that, and the man at the counter say's rather loud OIL BASE, AND LAUGHS, as to let everybody an ears length away know—we have a dork ordering paint. He takes me down the paint aisle, and sure enough there is no oil base paint where he is showing me, so he gets me to buy some latex semi gloss, which I'm thinking I have about 5 gallons at the house, but I'm really not quite sure, so when I arrive at home surprise—now I have 6 gallons. Maybe I can do the trim on my doors one more time! Back to the store—bought a toilet seat—I don't want to sit on a seat that's been sat on who knows how many thousand times—I mean even if you know the people.....do you really know the people? Got home opened up the new shiny toilet seat and guess what...no screws to attach the thing to the toilet. I bought some hinges at the same store, and every package had at least 5 to 10 extra screws—maybe I should call the toilet company, and they could hook up with the hinge company, and nobody would get screwed! Hold on now—went to the Depot, and have become very addicted—yes I know I'm a counselor, and I find myself excited that the one in Concord is open 24 hours a day....That's sick!! For date night Jane and I go out for dinner and for something to do…we head to the Depot. Can you imagine that all the things in that huge, giant store go in a house. I get so excited just walking down each isle, and every now and then I buy something because I think I need it, but when I get it home I don't, but they have the greatest policy for go backs…you go to the counter, and nobody hassles you— they just give you credit! (We all need someone to give us a little credit!) The thought of buying something just to bring it back…and experience the nobody hassling you for a mistake you made is a real good concept—I wish they had that at the store where I bought the hinges, because I didn't need all the hinges, but they made me go around the store buying things I didn't need until I had the right amount for fair exchange. What a hassle…now all that stuff is in the back of my jeep—maybe if I build another place in the next couple of years I will be able to use some of it. I'm not sure what I will do with the toilet seat with no screws…maybe make it into a nice picture frame -I saw one in Tahoe one time—looked good! Hey guys I know what the big thing about being a contractor is to the ladies now…Lean, tanned, and lots of money makes a good catch, but I have figured out a way to fool the women if you're looking for a good catch—First you have to smash—yes I said smash your thumb with a hammer real hard (real hard) like I did when I was nailing in some baseboard—yea missed the nail and WHAM—hit the thumb with all my might, and did the moon dance around the room for about 15 minutes. Next day it turned a real nice bluish purple. Now combine that with something I bought for the first time in my life…a carpenter's pencil…you know the fat square one. Put the pencil (sharpened) in your front pocket, (pointed end up) and when trying to get the pretty ladies attention make sure somehow you present the Blue thumb, and she will just assume that you are the contractor of her dreams and when her eyes wander down to your fat pencil………she is all yours…..and the rest is love and marriage.

THE COUCH POTATO

Let me tell you about my furniture adventure. Jane and I decided we would treat ourselves to a new couch, and Big Chair for our new place—well we went out looking and I mean WE, and I'm not really the type to go to a bunch of different stores and plop my buns down on hundreds of different couches, and chairs. I would pick the first one, but not Jane—NO we have to go sit on and in every available space that is not taken when entering a store! We pass this place by the Mall and it says on the window **HALF OFF EVERYTHING IN THE STORE!** Well you know that got my attention, and so we stopped in and began sitting on all the furniture, we asked the clerk to show us the selected ones that were "8 way hand tied," our friend Debbie told us they were the best….and like yourselves I had no idea what that meant, but it kind of gave us the edge like we knew what we were talking about (we didn't). We came to this couch and chair, (8 way hand tied) the guy even pulled all the pillows, and cushions off and asked us to come on board the couch standing and sort of jumping up and down, he says this is what they mean when they say 8 way hand tied-last forever. SOLD SOLD SOLD—Some of you might have seen me before—well I usually am weighing in at a solid 250 on a light day. He tells us this will last us 20 years, and I think to myself—20 years on the same couch could be just a bit boring but we say WE'LL TAKE IT! Now the fun begins—he tells us that if we want it just as it sits we can have it in 3 weeks—I do the math, and that's just a few days after we move in, so I tell Jane let's take it just like this, and she agrees. We leave the store very excited! Three weeks later we are in our new place with no living room furniture, because we gave it away—NOTHING IS IN THE LIVING ROOM except carpet, and a TV. Four weeks—NOTHING—5 weeks—NOTHING—6,7,8, NOTHING. Finally 9 weeks later a couch, and an ottoman arrive— we're excited—but where's the Big Chair? No-one seems to know, and our couch has a slip cover—we didn't order a slip cover couch (we think) it's been so long without a couch—who cares? After a few days Jane and I start asking each other—Aren't these arms kinda tall? Do you like this couch? Well we kinda decided we didn't, but hey we saved 50%, and did I mention it is 8 way hand tied? Towards the end of the week we decide to call the warehouse and find out if the chair has been brought in to the Country yet! (It has to be coming from somewhere very far away to take this much time) The sales guy—remember him? Well he assures us that it will be before we elect the new President (I should have known) well we ask him why he never mentioned the slip cover when he was selling us this great couch, and if the chair had a slip cover also. He says he'll get back to us—he did, and guess what—the couch we were sitting on for the last couple of weeks wasn't even ours—right material but wrong couch. It had been so long without one, and so long since we had bought it we had forgot what the one we picked out looked like. YOU GOT IT—WRONG COUCH! So where is our couch, and chair—who knows? They tell me that they are going to send someone over to pick up the couch, but I'm not giving up this one until I get mine!! Now 12 weeks later I got a call yesterday, and the lady says they are going to deliver my chair on the 30th. I ask her about my couch—she knows nothing, and says how is the Love Seat? I don't believe it—what Love Seat? I tell her about the mix up, and she says—I'll have to get back to you!….More next month!

Yes, it's true the couch has been delivered (the right couch). The 3 week delivery time only turned out to be around 17 weeks and two totally different couches. Let's see…in just that same amount of time my home has gone up about 20 grand, the electric company has filed for bankruptcy, Chad became more than a first name in Florida, Cheney had a stent put in his heart, Hillary became more powerful than her husband, Jesse Jackson added another child to his "or her" family which ever way you see it, Mayor Brown forgot to get married before he had his child—also—wait a minute Jesse is married, but has been for such a long time he must have forgotten. (old age)

LET'S PLAY DOCTOR

During this last month I had quite the wake-up call I needed—I was sitting in a meeting with the City when all of a sudden my chest felt like my new couch was delivered...on my chest. I asked the young gentleman sitting next to me if he knew CPR...he looked at me with a strange look and he said he did, and I said good...I believe I am having a heart attack. The ironic thing was I was waiting to get to speak, and I didn't want to leave until I got to get my point heard. Another scary thing crossed my mind...a lot of the people in the room have never really sat down with me to find out what I'm really all about, and my concern for the youth in this community and I felt that if I died in that room they would all be at my funeral talking about what a great guy I was and how much we had in common. For some reason people want to be the last person a dead person talked to just before they died. I did get my chance to speak, but I really cut it short, because I was so short of breath. On my way to the hospital I was hurting a lot more than usual and I was kind of scared. When I got to the hospital they whisked me right in, because I said heart attack. They immediately started giving me shots and pills and hooked me up on the EKG machine. I was having such a hard time breathing and my chest now felt like there was an entire furniture store on it. The nurse that was taking care of me was young and very pretty and was paying a lot of attention to my needs. I remember asking her for a few extra morphine shots to take the edge off. At one point the pain was unbearable and they gave me some nitroglycerin and it gave me a headache so bad I was wishing the heart attack would kill me. I can't remember how my wife found out I was at the hospital, but when she got there I was pretty far gone into the pain and the morphine. It seemed like the pretty nurse was making sure I wasn't going to die. She made sure the morphine was keeping me relaxed. OK I'm lying there thinking maybe I am dying and it seems that this nurse is kind of paying a little more attention to me than the rest of the patients. I'M KINDA FEELING LIKE SHE THINKS I MIGHT BE A GREAT CATCH IF I DON'T DIE- AND OF COURSE…. IF I WASN'T MARRIED. Jane asks me how I feel and what do I think happened and I tell her I'm fine and I'm sure it was an anxiety attack from being stressed out in the meeting and I should be getting out in about an hour or two. I guess she believed me because, she realizes that Christmas is a few days away and asks if I don't mind if she goes and picks up a few things and she heads to the Mall. The nurse comes in and asks where is your wife?...and I think I can sense a little jealousy. The doctor walks in and say's "where is your wife?" I'm wondering why everybody wants my wife. I tell them she had an emergency and had to go and then they hand me a bunch of paper and have me start signing on the dotted line. All of a sudden I am feeling like this might be more serious than I think. The first page of questions is about…if you die (yea die)…do you want your body parts given to others? The next is if you don't die…but become brain dead (like I'm not already) do you want the janitor to turn off the life support system? Well there are about 5 more pages and I'm really starting to think maybe this isn't anxiety or a locked in fart! Jane finally comes back just before they wheel me into surgery….. SHE FREAKS OUT when she finds out what is happening. Within minutes of her coming into the room I was wheeled away and rushed off to the emergency surgery room and they went into my heart and I got a stent, so I guess it was worse than we thought. The doctor tells me my main artery was a French fry away from a full blown heart attack. When I settle back into my room for the evening I am still really looped and I tell Jane about my friendly nurse…well she smiles, and asks "how much morphine have they given you"? I smile…Then she smiles again (I love my wife) then she tells me that the helpful young, pretty, and sexy nurse probably really misses her grandfather who is probably younger than

I am and I remind her of him. Sometimes I forget how old I have become (she burst my bubble) but I had a really great time with my fantasy while it lasted.

YOGA? IS THAT YOU?

I have got to tell you about going to our first Yoga class we went to at the Gym....I've been feeling real tight and thought this would be just what both Jane and I needed. So we go to the class that is on Tuesday night for beginners (I thought) we get there and there are a lot of people in the class and a lot of people we know so it was cool...the class starts and they turn down the lights and I was happy about that cause this was my first time...Well the stretching and pulling and the breathing was really fun and exhausting and made us feel really good....I had to laugh, because both Jane and I are not in the greatest shape. When I bend over to touch my toes (I can't) unless toes can grow out of knees. I hope you are getting the picture. At one point the instructor says ok now plant your left foot to hold yourself up and bring your right leg up and out and point it towards the wall...now walk your fingers down your leg and grab the bottom of your foot....keeping your leg straight...It's real quiet in the room except me breathing hard and making a lot of noises and grunting. I can barely grab the bottom of my feet with my knees bent all the way up to my chest...Now let's think about it.... Balance...and mobility are two things that I will probably never have...although I do see us getting a lot out of these classes...It might take a while, but it can't hurt (oh yes it can) my bones and my back and my legs and my ass all hurt the next day from one session...I've also heard that you can lose weight doing yoga...but if it is going to be this much work I'm going to try Pilates......there is way too much bending and maybe I should lose a bunch of weight before I get real serious about this......because my belly is so big it made it really hard to do some of the exercises. When you read this I will be turning 52...I would never have believed it.....Yoga at my age...It's all about quality of life...and mine is totally out of control...if you want to get healthy and be on the yoga team come join us....we'll see you at the gym...Breathe...Breathe...stretch... stretch...

THE STONES

Yep the stones....Let's start from the beginning..those of you who have been following my ailments over the last 2 years know that it's been a little rocky at best!! When I get a little stressed my heart or the area that it rests in..(it never rests) starts to hurt...the doctors say they can't figure it out...Yea I know.. (switch doctors). Well the other day I was out taking a picture of my clients George and Barb's house in Vallejo and while I was taking the picture it felt like all of my organs had decided to stop working as a team..it scared me because all that day my heart was not feeling its perky self..I looked at the lady of the house where I was at and made a few loud funny noises and noticed I felt like throwing up and passing out. I put the camera away and fell into my car after excusing myself and headed towards what I hoped was someone who could save my life...as I am driving off and Barb says are you alright to drive.... and I lie and say yea no problem. All of a sudden I was dizzy, sweating till I was soaking wet and I was in more pain than I have ever been in my life. Driving out of Vallejo towards Benicia I call my doctors office...when they answer.. I franticly ask if I can talk to the doctor.. the girl on the other end asks what's the problem...and I say "I'm not sure, but I think all of my organs have walked off the job and I'm dying...the girl on the phone seems a bit taken back and asks me to **"hold please"**..she comes back on the phone and says the doctor is in a meeting and not available and asks what is wrong with me again.. and I tell her I think I am dying if you know what I mean...it's the big one.. and she say's again **"hold please"**...that's it forget my doctor...I'm heading to the emergency room at the nearest hospital. At this point I'm driving down Highway 80 towards Benicia I've rolled down my window and I'm waving my arms at people driving by because I feel like I'm gonna pass out and crash so I'm trying to get their attention.... they look the other way and move away...they probably think I'm some drunk or something. I pull off the freeway and am stuck in traffic...at this point I have lost all dignity and am screaming at the top of my lungs in pain...I think I am dying...people are starting to move around me in their cars...I'm finally on the street that the hospital is on and the pain is way past my threshold of pain...and I know it's my last phone call so I call Jane and leave what I think is my last message. I pull into the hospital and can hardly walk.. I'm nauseated, I feel like I would rather just go now so I won't have to deal with the pain any longer...I make it inside and go to the emergency window..pick up the phone and the young girl asks.. what's my problem...I'm totally making as much noise as a man dying in pain, I'm soaking wet and delirious hunched over and I can hardly stay up on my feet...I tell her I think I'm dying because it feels like my organs have shut down...She asks me if I've been seen here before...I can't believe it..then she asks me my name...I tell her...I NEED TO SEE A DOCTOR I DON'T THINK I'M GOING TO MAKE IT...She asks me to have a seat..I'm so gone at this point I walk away from the window and go past the crowded waiting room where everybody is staring at me...I hear one person say..I don't think he's gonna make it..I hear the person she's talking to say...no I think it's just a heart attack..I go to sit down...the pain gets so bad I rush back to the window and am demanding to see someone before it's too late. She semi ignores me...I can only guess that maybe people do this when they come in just to be seen first...I DON 'T KNOW!! I am so convinced I am going to die I take the phone from its holder and start to smash it into the window where the lady is sitting all the while yelling I am dying. As I stand there I look into the window in the emergency room and see a bunch of doctors and nurses chatting and laughing...that's it I start yelling in pain and demanding help...I walk over to the double doors that the ambulance uses and start to kick at it and a nurse finally comes out and with a smile and tells me to calm down...you're hyperventilating and might pass out...NO..... I might die if nobody helps me...she asks me what hurts and where it hurts and I describe the pain and mention my heart problems and she says calmly....OH YOU'RE JUST PASSING A KIDNEY STONE...Yea right lady...... I don't believe her...because kidney stones are something I've heard about, but I always thought the guys telling me were big babies...If this is a kidney stone it must be the size of Half Dome..and if I'm not mistaken it has to come out of the end of my penis......I get a hospital bed and am still screaming in pain..they bring in the morphine...it doesn't change anything...they get more...no change....all the time I'm still screaming I'm going to die......I tell them I am going to throw up and they give me a pan about an inch deep and I hurl all over my hands and arms and the pan and the floor. Now I am in so much pain I start to beat the throw up pan with throw up going everywhere hard against the metal on the hospital bed. They come and give me more drugs. Finally the morphine is taking effect and I start to feel a little better......I think they should have not given me the last 2 shots......they just wanted me to shut up....drugged to the max...I'm being rolled down to X-Ray..When my wife finally makes it to the hospital (thinking I've Passed) intercepts my gurney in the hallway all hooked up with IVs and say's we have to go we're not covered here, as she tries to convince me to get off the gurney...I don't know what is going on and I really don't want to leave at the moment. I freak..then the nurse says.. it's an emergency and I'm sure it will be covered please let us get him to the x-ray dept....I am very relaxed and my wife is relieved I'm alive..after the x-rays we go back into the emergency room wait for a while and then they release me. My wife says I'll drive you home and I convince her to let me drive my own car, because I tell her I am fine....she goes for it and I can hardly drive, I feel like passing out every couple of minutes on the drive home, but I make it home and when I walk in the front door I collapse on the couch...and she freaks out....later on that same night I could feel more stones...I don't know if they have passed or they are going to wait for my vacation....I'll let ya know

SEND ME THE BILL, DOC

Let's start with the ending to the kidney stones visit.....They either came out while I was on Morphine and didn't notice, or while I was asleep, or they are waiting for a special day when nothing else is happening. Probably when I am in another country without a hospital for hundreds of miles. It was kind of funny that about a week after my visit to the hospital I received a survey in the mail from the hospital with questions about my visit....like how were you treated at check-in?...did you have to wait long? Well I did fill it out and was real honest...the only problem I really had was with the girl who should work at stamping Sunkist on oranges while they are still on the tree! Well I stapled the story from last month and hoped they could pass it around and get a few laughs.. *News Flash*....I got the bill for all that great service...$4,000...Let's see... that would be about $1,330 per hour. I have insurance but I didn't get a chance to show them my card. I have since called three times to give them my number and all I get is a recording...maybe they are trying to cut costs, so they can pay the doctors more...All I want to do is give them my HMO number....I already know what is going to happen...**maybe this has happened to you**......They won't get back to me....I will call many more times and get the same recording....Then they will send my bill to a collection agency and they will start hounding me on the phone and by mail telling me they are going to ruin my credit...and then I will finally get a hold of the hospital and they will tell me that I waited too long to pay the bill so they sent it to collections and it's out of their hands...So I pay off the **Mean People** who call all the time (who should also be stamping oranges) and they continue to send me bills with interest going up and no matter what I do this will continue for at least 6 months until the **Mean People** (who couldn't get a real job face to face with the public so they get jobs at these credit places making no money and not paying their own bills, so that they can sit on the phone and harass the public) it would be nice if the hospital and the collection company could get together at a meeting and someone could come up with a great idea....communicate with each other and *update the files.*

WORKING FOR THE FBI

Now for a little jaunt across the country...It's off to Boston...unlike my last trip to the East Coast this one was a lot different, because of the Sept. 11th. tragedy. This was my first trip in a plane since the airports have tightened up security. First off........I have to admit I was just a little scared...I know I'm a big guy, but I was scared...just a little. Everybody at the airport was under investigation....BY ME....I didn't let a person go by without evaluating what they might be up to and why would they be going to Boston. Yea even young kids with their parents.... I was thinking...maybe they really aren't kids....just disguised as kids. Well after making sure every person getting on my plane was checked over once or twice I focused on the pilots, and the crew. They all looked like they really worked for the airline......but you never know, but I relaxed a bit...always on guard though. I had a guy complaining about the long lines in S.F and I didn't say anything, but I was thinking......hey I don't really care if it takes all day..... I just wanna get there without anything crazy happening. Got up in the air and had a great flight...usually we fly First Class because our daughter is an employee for an airline...but it was full so we had to sit in business class and I was highly impressed...We were in the row just after 1st class and now they have to keep the curtain open so we are kind of in first class and a quarter...I don't think they thought that........but I did. The only thing that I noticed that they got that we didn't was the personal DVD player. Yea we had to watch the movie they wanted us to watch. The movie was "The Golden Bowl"....My wife likes these kind of movies...I can do without them, but I watched because it does take up a couple of hours of the flight. The flight was very uneventful not even your standard amount of turbulence. When we were landing the pilot comes over the loud speaker and informs us that there has been an "**incident**" on the plane and we all need to stay seated when we stop so "the incident" can be dealt with. Well my mind is racing...who is it...how did I miss them...is it the guy next to me?...wow you can just imagine...my little pea brain...was going crazy. The door of the plane opens and in come four large marshals with guns looking real serious....they come rushing in and stop in first class...It's the guy a few seats in front of us...I gave him a clean bill of health before he boarded the plane..I would have never guessed.....how could I have been so stupid....I would make a lousy FBI undercover agent....Heck I would make a bad security guard in the shopping mall parking lot. Well they ordered him to get up and asked where his baggage was and then escorted him off the plane....Pretty darn exciting.... I have no idea what it was all about...Just for a moment when the pilot announced there had been an incident...I thought **OH NO**.... did I do something to the flight attendant to make her mad.....or did I say something without realizing it...I've been told sometimes I run off at the mouth without thinking....(my wife lets me know) Well I'm glad it wasn't me. I wonder if he was the mad bomber, or maybe he just was an ass to the crew....that happens a lot when you are in first class....people thinking they are somebody because they are up front....I know all about the feeling.....I get that feeling when I fly first class.....I don't understand it, but it's real...

FRONT ROW

I have got to tell ya about going to see Elton John and Billie Joel—I had a prior engagement that was very high on the priority list but—hey how many times are these guys going to pass through town together?...probably never again. So I had to eat a little Humble Pie (that sure was a great band) to get to go.. but here is the kicker.....My buddy Ken calls and says "how would you like to go see Elton and Billie—he called and said he had tickets so close to the stage that if you know how to play a guitar...they will probably let you...well I can't play anything (I've always been more of a groupie) and I said OH HELL YEA I'LL GO. Then he tells me that the reason I get his wife's ticket is because she can't go because of the Reach Out board meeting that starts at 6:30...well I feel a little bizarre because—I'm the Director of the program and guess where I'm suppose to be? You got it...at the meeting, but Elton and Billie...come on!!!! Now let me tell you something...I have been invited to many concerts and if someone calls and says "were in the front row" I say smile and act all excited and tell stories about what we're goin' to do with the band after they play, and all the fun we will have when they invite us to their house for a weekend to just kick it with them, but don't forget to bring your binoculars so you will be able to make out who is the star and who are the players. I remember a long time ago George Harrison came to town on his "Give me Love, Give me Love, Give me Peace on Earth" tour...and I was so excited because my friends who bought the tickets told me that we were going to be so close George would probably ask us to join the band. Well we got there (Oakland Coliseum). He and Ravi Shankar were going to play and the guy who sang Nothing from Nothing leaves Nothing...Billy Preston. Well we walked in and proceeded down to the floor area towards the stage thinking we were so cool (we could put out a fire just looking at it) only to be stopped by the Bill Graham security. The guy looks at our tickets and kind of snickers and says, "you're not on this level...you are in row 1...and he points up to the ceiling in the middle towards the back of the building. Well I jump in saying "hey someone from the band helped us get these tickets, and they said we were going to get great seats." Well as we started up the stairs towards the highest level as far back as you could go (maybe this is where my heart trouble started) we got to our seats; wedged between the ceiling and the last row up. I remember when the band started I had gotten out of the bad mood and just figured I'd just groove to the music...well the band was playing and I said to the guy next to me "Isn't Harrison fabulous?"...and he says "That's not Harrison it's Ravi." So the story goes...Well I acted real happy about the front row with Kenny inviting me to see the show and that we would be right at the stage, but I also remembered George and thought about bringing the binoculars but I didn't want to make my buddy feel bad. Got to the concert and started showing our tickets to the attendants and there was a bit of confusion and it looked like I was right, but all of a sudden were up front with our hands on the stage, and when the concert started Elton and Billie walked out and asked Kenny and I if we wanted to come up on stage, but we told them it was their night and we just wanted to enjoy the show. We did and what a concert it was—They thanked us for showing up—knowing how busy we always are. I kind of sat a lot, but Kenny was up at the stage rockin out and every now and then I could see sweat fly off Billie and Elton's head and hit Kenny—we had a blast! It was nice to see a concert hall filled with people trying to look hip...even at the ripe old age of 60 or so.

OREGON RAIN OR NO RAIN!

We headed to the Oregon coast for a week of relaxation, but before we left I went on weather.com. What I found out will come as no surprise to any of you Californian's who have been to Oregon. RAIN, RAIN, SHowers, PARTLY CLOUDY, SHOWERS, AND RAIN. This was the weather report for the entire week we were supposed to be at the beach. I ask you….who in their right mind would head up the Oregon coast in September for a week on the beach to worship the SUN? Jane and Earl that's who…We were going to meet up with Jane's Mom and Dad and Steve my bro in law..and Diana the Sister in-law. I was bummed out for days thinking of all the places we could have been going…... Like Newport Beach California…not Newport Beach Oregon. I complained quite a bit about it to Jane, I guess you could say I am a whiiiiiner. Let me get something straight before we go on….I could live with Jane's Mom and Dad so that wasn't the problem…..SUN, SUN, SUN…I love the SUN and knowing that there wasn't going to be any….. I had to make a plan….I looked up the weather all the way up the California and Oregon coastal area and found that in Grants Pass Oregon the temperature was going to be 95' for a few days so I talked Jane into going up a few days ahead of the rainy coast trip. We had a blast along the Rogue River and it was very, very hot and I loved it. We just hung out at the pool the first day and soaked it all up….we headed over to this real nice park on the river to get more rays and as we were trying to find a spot to lay our blanket we noticed we couldn't find a spot to put down our blankets because there was DUCK, GOOSE and bird crap everywhere….. this must be the place they all fly to for a season….you had to walk between the crap that was like huge land mines. We found a couple spots...not next to each other but within yelling distance of each other....so we laid our blankets down and enjoyed the heat of the afternoon and just yelled back and forth.. On the second day we decided to go into Grants Pass and see if there was anything exciting to do...Hellgate Jetboat excursions....OH YEA!!! between 50 to 80 people get on this big boat and you haul butt down the river 16 miles. Sometimes the water is only about 6 to 12 inches deep, but this boat just glides right over and through the shallow water. This was a BLAST!....It was about a hundred degrees on the river, but the speed and the mist kept you semi-cool. As we were going down the river the driver asks us to hang on and with the boat going very fast this knucklehead spins a doughnut and at the end of the spin the water comes pouring in all over us. What a kick this was...I have a suggestion...we sat in the back row on an end...the water from the wake is at your fingertips to keep you cool...believe me you'll need it. Along the 16 mile stretch fishermen and fisherladies were all over the river catching salmon as large a small children, as we would go by they would hold them up for us to see....I was wondering if they were planted there to make us go home and make up fish stories, but some lady had a fish on...and the boat driver stopped and let us watch her pull this baby in. It took about 10 minutes it was as big as a first grader..and when she landed it everyone cheered....It was totally cool! Off to the beach and the theory...got to Newport Beach and it was hot and sunny...beautiful..the next day was the same...and the next day the same...and the next day the same...Hot and Sunny and beautiful...What a great vacation...OK now let's talk...Try my test...tell someone you are going to move or vacation in Oregon...what do they say? "It never stops raining in Oregon".... Heard it?...you bet you have...you probably tell the same story even if you haven't been there. My point exactly...The Oregonians have put together the best marketing plan in history....Tell everybody it's going to be raining if you come to Oregon...Even weather.com is run by Oregonians...They don't want us there and they have been lying to us for years...I think it is always sunny and hot in Oregon.

I think they have pulled off the best marketing scam the world has ever known. It ranks right up there with "it's a dry heat" what they say about Palm Springs........

LET'S GO TO PALM SPRINGS

I heard that come from my wife's lips and to tell you the truth… It was the last place I would have chosen to go on vacation…I had not really heard to many people talk about going to Palm Springs, so I just made up my own vision over the past 50 years… which was a bit off the mark..All I could imagine was people all around 50 to 70 sitting around a little flabby with suntanned dark skin and a lots of wrinkles….Hey wait a minute….That's me. So I gave in…only because she said we could spend the last two days of our vacation in Newport Beach. All I could imagine at the beach was silicone breasts and thong wearing hard bodies from Bay Watch everywhere you looked and at 52 this sounded like entertainment. Well we flew into John Wayne Airport…got a convertible Mustang…dropped the top and off we went…SMOG and more SMOG…what is with the people in LA…it looks like the place is on fire and nobody seems to care…We were coming up on a freeway exit and Jane said look at that mountain up ahead…and for the life of me I could not see it until we were on it! Well we drove towards Palm Springs and all of a sudden NO SMOG…beautiful weather and palm trees everywhere…it seemed like within just a few miles everything changed and now I know how they have kept the smog out…have you seen all the windmills…more than anywhere in the world…all the millionaires from palm springs bought them and pointed them at LA and they blow the smog back to LA. They tell you it's for electricity, but I know better. Got to downtown and I was totally blown away…This is paradise and the heat is a DRY HEAT…I would be walking along and people would burst into flames (not really). We stayed at a place called the DESERT HOUSE…a small hotel with 7 really awesome rooms in the heart of the village. Walk out your room a few feet away is the pool with the mountain right there (it doesn't get much better than this). Oh by the way...went to Newport Beach...no hardbodies, no thongs, no sun, no fun...I asked around and something I hadn't heard before was June Gloom. June gloom is what the locals called it...fog and cold weather most of the day.......It's the middle of the day and everybody is wrapped up wishing they were in Palm Springs....So did I...C-Ya there........

THE MAD BOMBER

The **Big Dig** in Boston? Well it's still alive and well...It's the biggest mess of...on and off ramps and turn-arounds, and tunnels you'll ever experience...If you are going to catch a plane...and you are driving your rent a car to the airport...you need to leave a week in advance if you are more than 40 miles away...and you still might be late. I had a scary experience at the Boston Logan Airport...Some guy left his luggage by the check in area and then split and all of a sudden cops were everywhere and when it was time to board...the security was intense and there were lot's and lot's of them with guns. Thick....they were everywhere...finally the guy who the luggage belonged to came up and security was ON him.... the guy whose baggage it was started yelling at all the security and telling them to shut-up and mind their own business....I was afraid the agents were going to pull out their guns and start shooting at this idiot....some of them had machine guns....who would start yelling and calling the 20 or so agents stupid unless you have something to hide. Now at this point I was certain that he was the **MAD BOMBER!** Our plane that is now boarding is now feeling kinda wierd...everyone getting on the plane is on edge...They finally search the guy...all his luggage...then they take him behind some curtains...and then bring him out and then a couple of them assist him to board the plane....Now..how do you think I feel about getting on the plane? Afll of a sudden I have taken on a new role of **The All American Hero**...If this guy comes up to the front of the plane...I am personally ready to **SUBDUE** him. I am the self appointed sky Marshall and I will not let anything happen to my flight or my people. This really made my plane trip home a whole lot uptight, but I was ready for anything up in first class. It made me feel a little better knowing we had that little curtain between us and him for our safety. It all ended up ok, but when I was getting off the plane I did feel like the American hero.

SURFIN' SAFARI

It's January 2003 and I don't know about you, but it sure seems like 2002 went by pretty fast....am I wrong or is it just me? I'm still kinda worried about the **millennium bug**...I think I still might have some boxes of cup of noodles and a bunch of bottled water in my garage along with enough batteries to light up the White House!! Jane and I just celebrated our **Ten Year Anniversary** and when I think about how fast the ten years went by....it seems to have been just about only a year or so....so what that means is that in about a year or so I'll be 63.........that's scary. **My life seems to be going by in dog years....** Speaking of Anniversaries..... We headed down the coast to go to **Mavericks....** down in Half Moon Bay for those of you who know what **Cow-a-Bunga** means...Mavericks is the talk of the surfer world. Mavericks wasn't really on the surfing circuit until 1990 and the news started traveling fast. In 1994 it produced one of the largest swells known to the California coast ever. Last year in November they say the waves were as high as 100 feet making Mavericks the place to be for experienced surfers (like myself). There is going to be the annual contest sometime between now and March 15th...For information on the contest and Mavericks...**www.MavericksSurf.com** If you are interested in heading over for the contest when it comes up...I'll be going so let's grab our boards and **(shoot the curl)**. Or maybe just leave the boards at home and enjoy the day watching those who belong out there!!!! Who knows......with a wet suit on someone might **mistake me for a killer whale and harpoon me**....then who would write these stories? The last time I tried to surf was with my two boys in **Santa Cruz about 15 years ago**....we rented boards, I dyed my hair white, we rented wet suits, got some wax and it was time to show my boys what I was made of...We headed over to Pleasure Point and got the wet suits on (mine was a little difficult, as I had gained quite a bit of weight and I'm sure it was made for someone 100 pounds and I was 250...**Have you ever seen someone in a wet suit that shouldn't be.....that was me!!** I also hadn't ever used the new short board before....I last headed out to surf on a Dewey Weber that was 10' 6" about 10 years before this day (25 years ago) We headed down the rocks to the beach with the boards and jumped in the water....what a blast this was going to be....I grabbed my board and laid on it to start paddling out and to my surprise **it sunk about 2 feet under the water**....a little embarrassed I explained to my boys that it was probably water logged....It was just that my body was water logged and I should have gotten a board about 15 feet long and 2 feet thick to hold me up....well that ended my **hot doggin** surfing day and my boys really never got to see me **hang ten or shoot the curl**.....but they did get to hear me use surfer lingo and tell lies about my surfing days all day until they were probably ready to throw up.....**Oh the good ole days!!!!**

JEEP CREEP

I am writing this in January and we did so many things already this month I am going to have to just highlight some of the crazy stuff. I don't know how many of you saw me at the intersection stop light coming off the freeway onto 2nd street up by McDonald's, but I was the guy in the green Jeep with the door open...stopped...broken down...mad...and wondering why with the light being green and my door open and my hazard lights on people were stopping behind me and honking. No they weren't honking to say hi they were honking to say get the hell out of the way...along comes this nice guy and says hop in and steer and I'll push...he must have looked me over and figured I might collapse if I was to push....moved the Jeep over to the side of the road...Do you remember that last month we forgot to pay the AAA bill after being with them for 10 years...this is the third break down since then and while we had the AAA I bet we only called them 1 time in 10 years.. It was great standing next to the Jeep waiting for the tow truck...everyone was yelling out...hey need a ride? Want some help...people were pulling over every few minutes...at one point two cars pulled over to help....One lady yells out "hey aren't you Earl? I love your cooking column"........I LOVE BENICIA!..... There was one guy who was a little bent out of shape that he had to wait about 20 seconds for the tow truck to back up when it got there and he let us know by yelling out his window and flipping us off. If that was you and you are reading this.... could you do me a favor and come to my office at Coldwell Banker on First street...I would like to hold that middle finger for you! Well I go to pick up my Jeep at Gotelli's and Gene tells me even though he loves that I have a Jeep and it is costing me an arm and a leg and a few more checks out of my check book....he wants me to get rid of it because he and his beautiful wife have gone on too many vacations on my repair bills and they would like to spend more time with their granddaughter at home. So I head off to buy a used SUV.....I go to a friend's dealership in Concord....He puts me with a smooth talking fast walking sales-dude and the next thing I know I am leaving the lot in a brand new Tahoe...You could say I was caught up in the moment. I got a great deal...I think...and the sales-dude was slick as teflon....I can honestly say the best thing about buying a new car was I got to wave bye-bye to the Jeep.

REDMAN

Last time we talked we were headed to New York and New Hampshire....Well we were watching the weather report over the weekend and decided the cold would be too much for our tired old bones........so we headed to Maui...Lahaina...the Hyatt on the beach....Now we're talking...instead of 25 we got 85...since winter started I've gotten a whole lotta white...so the first day we hit the lounge cabanas on the beach and I laid there all day to soak up the sun....someone mentioned Sunscreen.....No I'll use that tomorrow...I always feel like it will block to much sun from frying my body.....Well guess what?....You got it...Lobster face..."What an Idiot...I told you to use the 48 sunscreen...how many times do we have to go through this...for you to get it?" Is it that you just want some cancer to get some attention?...Smart words from my wife. My nose was so sun burnt it was bleeding...I know...I know....I know...next time. The next day I was known as RED MAN around the pool...I don't know how they could tell I was red..I was in full towel dressing around my head and body....the red must have been shining through the towel. I swear never again.

BASKET CASE

First off let's talk about my costly vacation to the shopping center. Went to the store to pick up some ice and sodas for my group on a Monday for that evening. I was putting the ice in the ice chest to cool down the sodas for the youth I heard someone yell "YOUR BASKET" and to my surprise as I looked, up my basket was heading down the parking lot picking up speed and by the time I started after it the basket was doing about 55 miles an hour. I ran after it, and reached out to stop it from ramming into a new Toyota Camry, but I was a little too late…. **BAM**…I looked around, no one was looking and I could have gone back to my car and headed home, but I believe that we should always do the right thing. So I looked over the car and noticed that the basket had cracked the tail light, as I sat there waiting for the person to come out of the store from shopping, many things were going on in my head. I waited a little while, but no one was coming to the car, so I went back to my car to get a business card and a pen…. I have hundreds of business cards but I had no pen, so I couldn't leave a note…I thought of going inside and getting on the loud speaker "attention would the person who owns the gold Camry with the smashed tail light please come up front to the check stand…. the guy who let his basket go that hit your car is waiting for you," but I thought that would make someone even madder. I waited a while longer and this lady comes out to her car and I say…"Hello, is this your car?" she looks startled and she says yes so I tell her **my basket hit your car.**… I described what had happened and I gave her the information needed and told her I would get it fixed for her…not to worry…. **and it was just at that moment I realized that I didn't own a basket**…so how could My basket hit her car…it was the supermarket's basket that hit her car.... if it were my basket I would have put brakes on it so when I was away from it, it wouldn't roll. So I went into the store to find the owner of the basket.... He was in a meeting, so they say. I left my name and address...I never got a call, but I did call Gotelli's Garage and found out that for a good citizen discount at only $226.00 I could clear my mind of all wrong doing. I set up the drop off and pick up of her car without using the insurance company, because you know what I would have gone through. It felt really good to do my part as a good citizen and we both lived happily ever after. I have a question for you now.... **should I be the new owner of the basket?**

BATES MOTEL?

Yet another trip to Boston and New Hampshire.....I took a late flight and first class was filled up but they gave me the first seat behind first class and there was actually more room and now that I don't eat everything in sight it was good not to get a full course meal. I got to Boston at 11:30 PM and got to the rent a car place at about midnight which I knew was only 9 pm in California, so I thought it would be a good idea to head up to my hotel in New Hampshire. I have complained about the Boston Airport reconstruction enough in the past so I'll just say this.... everyone that has had anything to do with the project called the "Big Dig" should be arrested. So I get to the Car Rental place and wait at the counter a bit when this nice smiling gentleman comes out..and out of his mouth comes a bunch of words and the only ones I understand are...I'm from Africa. I told him I ordered an SUV and he says...we don't have any...Hey...I have already paid for an SUV I tell him...he doesn't seem to care much...he points out into the lot and says...go see if you like any of those. So I go get in a Rendezvous...it's not bad...it's a little weird looking, but hey no one will see me in it...so I go in and tell him OK....As I'm leaving in the car I notice on my paperwork the car I'm supposed to be driving is not the one I'm in. I pull back into the parking lot and go back in and explain what he did and it really doesn't matter because I can't understand him anyway. He gives me the keys to the vehicle that he did the paperwork for and I go out into the parking lot again and I get out all the luggage and put it all in the other vehicle and head out of Boston. The way out of town is through the Sumner tunnel...I get to the Tunnel and it's closed....there is a cop there who points the other direction and smiles....I bet this is the first time in 50 years that the tunnel has ever closed. I don't know any other way out....I start to circle the area and get real lost....I end up going up the coast highway until I see this Limo driver in a gas station...I ask him to direct me to the Highway I need and he sends me back to Boston....Now it's almost 1:30 and after a bit I find the right Highway. AHHHHHH....I'm on my way...remember the hurricanes that hit last month...well I was driving through the storm as it hit the East Coast...Rain...I mean real hard rain...no visibility rain...Pain in the Butt rain..It's a good thing I was the only one on the road. Now it's getting late and I feel like I might have made the wrong turn...as I head down the road towards my folks house...I'm lost, mad, tired, frustrated, and I'm flying down this old county road and I stumble upon this sign with my hotels name on it....it must be a miracle....I screech to a stop and go in the parking lot....It looks closed...only 2 cars in the lot and there are 50 rooms....Great advertising......I park and go to the front door..I had called earlier and told them I would be late, so they told me they have left a key for me in the mailbox. I put the key in the lock and guess what? It doesn't work. It's now pouring...I mean pouring...I run around the outside of the hotel looking for another entrance and there isn't one. I run back to my car to turn it around and shine the lights on the front door to see if I can get the key to work, and maybe wake someone up. I put the key in and the car doesn't start...Oh My My...I try everything...nope...It's not going to happen...I get my phone out and guess what....It's dead...I decide to sleep in the car.. I can't believe this is happening...I put the seat back and start to relax, but I'm so mad I can't even think about sleeping...So I try the keys again...guess what...I have 2 sets of keys...remember the car I was leaving the rental lot with...Yup I took the keys...I bet they were going out of their minds looking for them. I put in the right keys and turned the car towards the front door and shined the lights on the door and to my surprise....On the key chain they left me... there are 2 keys....I get in the hotel and out of the rain and I am dead tired and need to get some sleep. I get in and I'm going up and down the hallways and I can't find my room...Nobody anywhere....

Finally....Room 35 my room. I am so happy to find my room and I go inside and turn on the light. Oh my this place was built in the beginning of time and they haven't changed a thing...not even the beds or the quilts...I curl up in the 5 foot long bed with the wood foot board so I can't stretch out...It's time for me to get a little shut eye....Now that it's 4AM...and I am WET and tired. I have a friend Rocky who told me what Rustic means....OLD PIECE OF CRAP!! Exactly what I checked into. A few hours later I wake up...I got about 3 hours sleep....and I go downstairs.....The guy at the desk smiles and say's good morning Pearl...I don't respond...All I can think of is...........Norman is that you?

IS IT JUST ME?

Let's talk about my medical condition....I'm feeling pretty spunky at 53, but I always keep in mind that **my heart has a man- made tube in it** to keep the blood flowing. I don't know about you, but I've had quite a few things over the years that were made by man that were far from reliable. I don't really trust man-made things...after all I have owned quite a few broken down autos, cell phones, message machines, watches, coffee makers...well you get it...these things all broke and were made by the same people who made my tube. I'm now 60 pounds lighter than last year and you would think my blood pressure would be stable...**not**...I don't know if you are all up to speed with ordering your medicine on-line, but I have __no time__ so I ordered my blood pressure pills on line with enough time in advance so I wouldn't run out...because they tell me you can't stop taking them once you have started....**Who Made This Rule UP?** So as my pills were running down to the last few...I'm jogging out to the mailbox and checking the mail each day...now just the thought of running out is sending my blood pressure up where is shouldn't be. Now it's really getting scary.....OK now we are down to one pill...I can already start to feel my heart hurting...I don't know if it's just cause I'm a freak, or maybe there is something going on. I go on-line and I get an e-mail from the hospital and they send a letter saying **"we are sorry"**...we didn't get your medicine out, but we are going to mail it to you today...at no cost, because of our mistake...I am now 5 days into not taking medication and... just maybe it's all in my head, but it feels like someone has pushed a pencil right through the center of my heart. I go to the mail box because (they promised) it would be there. I call and tell my dilemma to the hospital and they tell me to come right down to the pharmacy and I can get my pills...I take off and head to the hospital...I get there to wait in line for quite awhile...**blood pressure rising**...I try to stay far enough away from everyone in line cause their all sick. I get to the counter and the girl says **NOPE** we're out of those...come back tomorrow...I tell her that I had just got a call to come to the hospital and pick up the pills. I tell her my heart hurts and I would like to take something similar so my heart doesn't stop...she looks at me like I am her pain in the ass for the day and she walks up to the window and yells back to the pharmacist and he sticks his head out of the window and say's OH these aren't for pain...**No kidding Einstein**. I tell them I'm not leaving without something and they tell me my prescription will be in a few days...and they can give me 5 pills to take while I'm waiting for mine. I tell them that would be fine and I show her the letter and how it says the prescriptions will be no charge and she say's that will be $16.00...for the 5 pills. I ask her...what part of the letter did she not understand? She say's "that is for your prescription not the 5 replacement pills." Now my blood pressure is at the point where **I feel like someone removed the pencil and replaced it with a railroad spike**. I pay...so I don't die on the spot. They said they would call me when my pills were in...I call them on the 5th day as they seem to have forgotten to call me....**I go in and wait in line**...get up to the counter and give my hospital card and the letter...the girl say's we just got some of those in, but yours have been sent in the mail...**BLOOD PRESSURE.. ALL TIME HIGH!** I explain the story and tell her I'm not leaving without my pills...she has me move over and away from the counter and she will talk to the pharmacist.. in the meantime the next lady in line is getting her pills and when she is done then the next lady moves up to the counter and the girl says ok Mr. Miller...I try to move back into position at the counter and the lady who was next in line won't move...**BLOOD PRESSURE RISING!** The girl looks at me and gives me a head signal to wait a little more and takes care of the lady and then she finally leaves. I move up to the window and start to talk to the girl and she asks for my card, but she had taken my card already...I tell her she took it and she looks at me like I'm lying...then she says that the lady who wouldn't move must have taken it...then she says...that's her right there go get your card....I walk over and ask the lady if she was just at the window and she says no...I freak out and I start asking every lady in the pharmacy...**NO way am I going through this....I can't believe it**...I go into the hall and start asking every woman...she's gone..I go back to the counter **BLOOD PRESSURE AT ALL TIME HIGH and heart about to burst!** The girl say's you will have to order another card...I say NO...you will have to order me one...then she says...the pills will be 20 something dollars. I ask what about the letter...she say's "who is the letter from? **I can't believe this is happening...**I tell her to give the letter to the phaRmacist...she does and he pokes his head out the window and say's NOPE you have to pay....I was ready to jump over the counter and start hurting people, but I felt that in a few minutes the blood was going to stop flowing in my heart and the man-made tube was going to explode..so instead of dying in the pharmacy I paid the money and left the hospital.

PARTY BARGE

OK...It's September...well I think it is...OK it is! That means just 3 months to Christmas.....I find that hard to believe...how about you....does time seem to be flying by at warp speed? Was there a summer? Did you get to go to all the places you wanted to....I barely had a good tan all summer. I think when you get older you just lose time and it goes by without you really relaxing in it. One thing I did this summer was take my boat out...you know the one that only goes about 7 or 8 miles an hour. It's a party barge...I thought when I bought it that it was going to be an excuse to go party for a few days at a time. NOT........ since I bought the boat I think my friends have had more time on it than me. I loaned it to a friend last month to go to Shasta...I told him ahead of time that it only went 8 miles an hour tops.....with no wind....well he brought it back to me and I took a day off to bring it back up to where I dock it in Middletown. As I was leaving Benicia I was looking at the mooring cover and thinking........Am I suppose to take it off when I drive or leave it on? Well I was going on the freeway at Fifth Street and it looked OK, but I asked Jane.... do you think we should be driving with the top on? She said "I don't know" and I said....well they call it a mooring cover...so maybe it should just be on when the boat is mooring. Well I see a lot of boats going by with their covers on so....no big deal...as we are having the conversation I looked back in the rear view mirror and YUP... the top was ripping to shreds and waving all over the freeway. I stopped and whooooooooooooa.......no more mooring cover....just about 4 or 5 mini-mooring covers.........took it off and headed back on our journey. Maybe next time....no never mind....there won't be a next time......I'm selling the party barge....I'm all partied out...If

I figure what I spent on the boat and how many times I've been on it...it comes to about $1,000 per hour. I think I can find some other kind of entertainment that would cost a lot less......like sitting down at the marina watching boats go by drinking a Pepsi and just having a good chuckle and quiet little party by myself. I guess next time I get a wild hair brain idea.....maybe just maybe I'll think about it for more than a minute.....probably not. I can honestly say I haven't jumped on the surf board buying trip quite yet....boy I'm close, but I really have been giving this some thought.

RIVER DANCE

It's summer time and the livin' is easy! Who made up that line? Probably some rock star! I'm working more hours seven days a week and watching everyone stress about going on vacation. Well we haven't gone on vacation yet...a lot of my friends tell me I'm always on vacation. It must be the Hawaiian shirts. A lot has happened since last month and I'm happy to say...**I have 3 months of blood pressure medicine**. Have you seen the movie Pirates of the Caribbean? I kind of did...yea.. I was there at the theatre, but because of the luck of the draw I always seem to get stuck in a seat in front of the weirdest folks on the planet. I sat in front of a guy who seemed to be practicing for a job with River Dance. This guy was tapping his feet...and it seemed to be that he was tapping on my head. The new seating at the theatres is really great unless you have someone behind you who #1 Brings his own food from home in noisy bags. #2 Talks all through the movie. #3 A person whose laugh is made up and so loud you would tell him to shut up if you knew him. #4 Someone who taps his feet all through the movie. **THIS IS THE GUY SAT BEHIND ME!**...I sat minding my own business until this guy started to tap dance on my seat and then I would look back at him "with the look"...you know.... like knock it off buddy or I'll....whoops...this guy looked mean and I am getting older...so I would just look...Not the...I'm gonna kick your butt look, but kind of.... would you let the old man please watch the show in peace look. **NOPE it just made him tap more**...at one point I looked back and it seems that his girlfriend was kind of laying on top of him...but he was still tapping. I think he was tapping and humping at the same time. I really wanted to get up and just stare at him and start yelling, but everyone else was into the movie and they probably would have yelled at me. Then it happened...he started tapping on my seat...just slow one every minute or so taps...NOW I really want to rip this guys legs off...I think he just didn't like me...**Maybe he knew I was a Realtor** or maybe he didn't like his dad or Grandpa and he was taking it out on me...Who Knows?...but all of a sudden a strobe light goes off in the theatre and everyone starts to scramble....It's the fire alarm.... the guy behind me jumps up with everyone else and they all start for the doors...**NOT me....I'm going to get a few minutes of the movie without the DORK behind me tapping on my chair...** I'll wait till I'm half burned...I'm going to get some of my money's worth of the movie. All of a sudden the isles are full with people trying to get out and people start yelling at each other...a small panic sets in....I want to tell them to "shut-up can't you see I'm trying to watch the movie", but they we're getting hostile. Then the strobe light goes off and there is a sigh of relief with the crowd...and people start to sit down again...I see the tapper heading back to torture me, but the strobe light comes on again and he retreats.... I'm thinking......."Chicken" "scared of a little fire are ya?" but I get back to the movie...then the light goes off...everyone in the isles just stands there dumbfounded....Especially Michael Flatley...the movie is about to end so everyone stays standing except me and Jane.... we just sit and enjoy the end of the show.. After the movie is over we walk out and I see the tapper, but he doesn't seem to notice me...maybe he wasn't trying to annoy me...maybe he was just the nervous type...like me! Oh well....**he did ruin my movie**....As we rounded the corner I noticed all the people from our show standing in a line...They were passing out free passes for everyone who was in our show....for the false alarm...I kind of knew it was a false alarm...that's why I didn't jump up so quick...You gotta think that at least one employee from the theater would have come in to tell us to get out....and no one did...but then I think....did you look at the people helping out front? If there was a fire would they risk their lives for us? **I think not!** The guy who I got my popcorn from wouldn't say you're welcome...I said loud and clear two times

THANK YOU...no reply so I said it again **THANK YOU**...and he just looked at me like I was speaking another language.....I will give him the benefit of doubt though......He could have been deaf or he might have never heard it at home...Maybe they should teach it at the popcorn training school?

WEDDING BELL BUDGET BLUES

O K. It was time to join all the other families who I have heard talking over the years about their daughter getting married. My beautiful daughter got married last month and it was rather a long time coming. She is 31 and her husband is 43….Well at least they are telling me he's 43…who knows…I can hear ya now…oh that's too old for her….well I said the same thing… remember I'm 53…he is actually closer to my age than hers…but I'm already taken. That brings us to Jane…Yup…the mother of the bride….Let's start from the beginning….when Jodie and Rick sat in our living room and told us of their plans I was real happy and being the tight wad I am, at times I was also a little concerned. Thoughts were racing through my head of going broke. Would I not be able to buy a Harley this summer? Is the boat purchase out?…what about my vacation? I have heard horror stories about the costs of weddings nowadays. Every time our daughter was over to the house for the last year or two she would park herself in front of the TV and watch the wedding shows. Sometimes I would sit and watch with her…. I don't know why….I would even catch myself crying over someone else's wedding…..usually about the cost. Now I have to tell you…I talked to quite a few of my friends around town and asked for advice about what I should spend. I needed to tell the kids about how much money I was going to spend. You wouldn't believe some of the things people would tell me. Everyone has an opinion about the wedding subject…"what do you mean pay for their wedding….they are too old to have you pay"…."He's been married before…well then let him pay"…."How much money does he make?" "Why don't you give them $5,000 and tell them to go to Vegas." "Whatever you do put them on a budget"…….out of all the things I had heard that sounded like a great idea! OK so here I am...I want to be the good guy, but I also don't want to go broke by letting go of my control. My wonderful wife says "I have always told Jodie I would pay for her wedding"....and I'm thinking..."**Then why don't you?!**" But, I kept that to myself...'cause you know that divorce is even more expensive...So we sit down and I have already put a number in my head of what I think it should cost...they kind of laugh and tell me if that's it then "we are going to have to lie to you about what we spend"...and I think....go ahead and lie, it might make it better...but I stick to my figure and tell them to put it all down on paper...I saw that on the wedding shows...and a budget...yes I said budget....OK now I'll give you a little background on my wife and her daughter...neither one of them have ever kept a running balance in their checkbook, so who was I fooling? I told them I was going to put the money I thought was fair in a separate bank account....and I did. From that day forward things kept coming to the door everyday in packages on a day by day basis...big boxes...little boxes...long boxes...lots of boxes...and I had a feeling they hadn't wrote any checks for this stuff. There were shopping sprees, and showers.... did I say showers? Excuse me...I counted about five showers...and something new...a wedding Tea...who thought of that? What it all means is five dresses for my wife....and don't forget the shoes... How about a bachelor and bachelorette party...and then separate parties...and how about a bachelorette party in Monterey with spa treatments and all kinds of other fun things...OK...I was getting a little paranoid when I would ask...are we on budget? I would get the deer in the headlights look and then "Oh yea....everything is on track".... I think American Express knew about the wedding, as I think I heard them ask Jane on the phone one day...how it was going. Well it was coming time to have the wedding and I quit asking and quit counting...I did keep bitchin' though! In the end it was only about double the budget...maybe triple....I think...I will really never know what the total was, but in the end I could have cared less...to be blessed with the greatest daughter on the planet and oh yea don't forget the new old dude!

STRESS CASE

For all of you that have been keeping up with my medical escapades over the last ten years I have some new news! **They think I'm a stress case.** Imagine that. OK I admit I do stress out about things here and there, but not to the point to where it disables me. OK well at least I didn't think so until last year when I was spending enough time at hospital that even the security guards and janitors knew me by my first name. Last year was a very busy and a tough year...I was running a non-profit substance abuse organization seeing 25 to 50 youth a week...I was being a husband...I was teaching at a High School...I was writing this column for the Weekender and a recipe column...also I had a private practice counseling service office with patients..I was a Grandfather.. A Father..A Son..A Friend to many...I was in my first year of Real Estate sales...and it was going wild with interest rates the lowest in 40 years...I was going to meetings...a lot of meetings...I was going to church...I was going to prisons...speaking at schools and different organizations...I was putting on benefits and a few more things to boot. Now I ask you......Doesn't everybody have a full day? Now some people tell me that I do too much and move to quick...I just can't see it...a lot of the time I'm bored and wonder what to do with all my extra time. A few years ago I had about ten weeks where I didn't know what to do with my spare time so I painted pictures about fourteen of them for the whole ten weeks and haven't painted since (too busy). Well I am here to tell you...maybe all the fuss is worth looking into. The other day I was feeling real good and all of a sudden it felt like someone shoved a pencil through my heart...Not a good feeling...I really didn't pay much attention to it, because I was to busy, but the pain wasn't going away...at first

I thought it was all in my head…Nope it was all in my chest! I didn't tell anyone, because I didn't think I had enough time to sit at the hospital all day. It seems that the hospitals are busier than ever these days. I would rather let the sick people get help…and if I did go check in just think how long the really sick people would have had to wait then. So I just go about my day…a few people mention that my color is off and I say "you bet it is…I haven't been out in the sun for a couple of weeks." As the day progresses though I start to have a little trouble…Yes a little…trouble breathing…could be the start of a cold…or the flu…Well I go home at the end of the day and go to bed…I wake up in the middle of the night and it feels like someone is trying to pull the pencil out of my heart…I think to myself…this is not good…..do I want to wake up my wife?…she really needs the sleep and has a big day at work tomorrow…Nope I will just get up and go watch some TV. I am watching TV and the whole time I am thinking I am having a heart attack. Well if you know me…you know that it takes something pretty big like a car accident or falling out of a building from ten stories high to get me to the hospital…It was getting into the next day and I was feeling **not so good**…and my wife reminded me that I had just gotten Life Insurance…. **and I probably would be just fine**…Do you think she was thinking about collecting on me? The whole life insurance thing made me think I better get to the hospital, so I got in my car and I rushed over to the hospital. It really wasn't the insurance thing that made me go…I decided I better go because I have a vacation coming up and I didn't want to miss it!! I get there and there are about 25 people in the waiting room…..all sick! I go to the window and the lady asks **what seems to be the problem?** So I say…well if feels like someone has just rammed a pencil into my heart and I am getting dizzy and feel like fainting and my left arm is asleep and I'm having a hard time breathing…..She say's…have a seat and someone will be calling you. Yep…I was the next one called…about a minute after I checked in….They probably realized how busy I am and wanted to get me back to work..In just a few minutes…I'm all hooked up with EKG wires all over my chest…things on my fingers, a little robe and an IV hook-up in my hand ready to feed me drugs and food and stuff. Well I'm lying there off in my own little emergency room and nobody is paying any attention to me and all of a sudden my phone rings...well I can't get to it because it's in my pocket and the IV thing is making it impossible to get to. The IV thing is really hurting because to get to my phone I have to bend the needle back a little bit..Ouch Ouch Ouch......Oh Yea...finally I get my phone...It's the Benicia Herald and they want to ask me some questions...well all of a sudden the nurse comes around the corner and into my room and sees me on the cell phone and with a real weird look on her face has a small little fit...I guess the heart monitor machine went wild when I answered the phone and they thought I was a goner....Nope I was just taking care of business here in my relaxing bed all wrapped up in warm blankets with nothing to do but talk on the phone. It was then I started to realize my problem...I am just too busy..... I do need to slow down...So for now on I'm going to take all of my calls when I'm in bed...

AIRPLANE RIDE FROM HELL

What is it with me and airplanes? And me and the weather? Last month I had to take a trip to Las Vegas...to a drug and alcohol education convention....I know that seems weird, but it's true. What better place to get educated about drugs and alcohol? The only other education missing in Vegas would be prostitution and gambling. When I took off, it was suppose to be about 75 in Vegas...Now if you have been reading my stories over the last few years...I have a strange feeling I could be the reason for bad weather all over the globe...I'm seriously thinking about changing my name to Earl Nino. So when I get to Vegas I just start walking around apologizing to everyone I meet. Up in the airplane (yes..again) the weather started to change......FAST......dark, windy,...the pilot comes on the intercom...just like my flight to LA last month and says.....everyone, even the flight attendants, please be seated and buckle up for some rough ride as we are coming into some heavy turbulence....TURBULENCE...this was not turbulence...this was a hurricane up in the air....this was sheer terror. The plane started doing things like dropping down 20 to 30 yards at a time...which seemed like miles...then it would stop and shake and shimmy and then get swept up just as fast. I thought the wings were going to rip right off....(ladies were screaming) I looked around and it seemed that everyone had out their throw-up bag...this is the first time..... I really thought we weren't going to make it....I started thinking about my life...all of it...in a matter of seconds....I wasn't ready to go down....next to me was this what looked like about a 15 year old with spiked hair totally cool dude with head phones on (groovin) so when the plane would drop he would look at me and he seemed to really enjoy it and I would smile and act cool....like we were on some roller coaster ride at an amusement park.....all the while I was praying for GOD to help us.... and that he would carry us to safety...the young guy kept looking at me and smiling every time we would drop or shake.....I just kept smiling...I really felt helpless and scared, but at one point I felt like putting my hands in the air like we were on a roller coaster (for the kid, to show him how cool the old man was). I was wondering what everyone would say at my funeral if we went down...then I would get weird thoughts like... who would finish the weeding in my backyard...it was scary and I just wanted it to be over....well we made it to the ground...once we had landed and rolled towards the gate, everyone clapped, as if we had just cheated death and then there was this huge loud sigh of relief...when I was leaving the plane and I went by the pilot...I thanked him..as if he had just saved my life....he had...it felt great to walk on solid ground again, but I didn't think much about it after that. From now on I will be going on weather.com to find out the weather report before I book any flight...and I'm also going to get that flight insurance you see at those machines on your way to the gates. I probably could have handled the whole episode a lot better if it weren't for the cool teenager and the ladies screaming.

24 HOUR VACATION

OK let's talk about the 24 hour vacation...some of you have seemed interested in trying our idea out. I have got to tell ya.....it really works. Now, I know a lot of you are kind of on a vacation all the time, but for those of us with a double schedule this is the best thing going. A car dealer friend had called and asked if we would like to try out one of the new sporty Cadillacs for the weekend. Knowing if we liked it we would probably buy it. So we drove up to the Sonoma area and slipped into the Sonoma Mission Inn for another one of our 24 hour vacations. It was an anniversary getaway.... Plus a friend had given us a gift certificate for $350 so we thought we would use it up and treat ourselves! Now I know that stuff costs a little more in Sonoma, but just wait a minute.... I even thought we would have a little money left over for dinner. (I was thinking the room to be about $150—Massage $100—which leaves $100 for dinner.) We got there and we walk in to the lobby and everyone is in robes...real nice white robes...felt kinda weird knowing everyone had nothing on underneath them...like a sexy grownup pajama party...which I am totally not against, but it did seem weird...checked in.. and then got escorted to our room...which Jane picked out....walked in and **WOW**...it was breathtaking...a **Huge room** and a **Huge bathtub** in the middle of the room right by the bed...I mean this is **a Sweet "Suite"** a beautiful living room with fireplace, refrigerator, wine and champagne on ice....I started to think.....maybe this might cost a little more than I expected...well I went to the closet to hang up my Hawaiian shirts...I always bring 3 or 4 in case I need to change a few times in a day. As I am hanging up my shirts and I see the piece of paper that has the room charge that usually changes season to season....there is no season change here…just $569.00 a night…I almost faint…I don't say anything because Jane set this year's anniversary getaway up. We get all cozy and naked and put our robes on in the room and head down to get our massages…The message package Jane picked is called the wine and roses…couples massage. We get led to the steam room… then the hot pools, there are other couples in the tubs with us, but everyone is being very quiet in the huge bubble tub, it's heaven… then someone comes to get us to go to our room….Oh my…we walk in and there is this brass tub…huge….**really huge tub**..filled with bubbles…I mean a few feet of bubbles and rose petals all over the bubbles and all over the floor and everywhere…..Unbelievable….we jump in the tub…Jane's sipping wine…and me, I don't know what I'm sipping but it's good…water with cucumbers and flowers and herbs.. In just a little while the two women masseuses come back in the room and we get up on the massage tables and for the next hour and a half…..rub a dub..dub. When we walk out I'm feeling so relaxed and care free…I'm thinking this just might cost more than the $150.00 I had thought at the beginning……So I ask Jane.. what does something like that cost? Trying to make her feel like…. no matter what the cost.. it was definitely worth every penny..at this point I do not want to rock the boat…just for reference…You know just in case any of my friends would like something like this…she says with a smile $450.00…and all of a sudden I tense up and my body goes into shock and I feel the big one coming on thinking I better get back to our room to get the hospitals phone number……. OK let's get this right….our little 24 hour get away…Room and massage.. is over $1,000 so far…and we haven't gone out to eat or shop yet! OH MY GOD!….I'm thinking let's forget the shopping.. and let's find a McDonald's. All I can say is that next year when it's my turn to plan the next Anniversary you can bet the only one rubbing me will be Jane.. and just for the romantic side of it….we will stay in the spare bedroom at our house. Heck I'll even buy her a bottle of Andre' Brut.

FACE ON FIRE

It's been kind of a quiet month….. except for the screaming and heavy breathing, because of a **facial fire…**and the anxiety attacks. OK let's start with going to the spa to get relaxed and have a shoulder and neck massage, because the whole month I was a little tight!! **Did I say a little tight?** The muscles on my shoulders looked like I had baseballs implanted under my skin. Jessica who was giving me the massage stopped at one point and said she didn't think it would do any good to continue……**You are very tense!**….. she was right, because all I can think about when I'm getting a relaxing massage is who is trying to reach me on the phone when I'm just laying there doing nothing. It was Jane's idea to go to get a little unstressed…..Now I got to tell ya…….I love a good massage, **but now my wife has talked me into a facial…**yes I know….doesn't seem very macho….but there really is a softer side to me. My wife tells me that my face has been wrecked by the sun. Sometimes when I look in the mirror I do see a real resemblance to **the giant Iguana.** OK, I'm laying on the table….the soothing music is playing…..I'm not sure if there was a little fountain with the bubbly waterfall, but you all know what I'm talking about. OK so now **Jessica** is in the middle of my facial……..which is soothing and relaxing to say the least….then she starts with what I call the **sand scrub**….I don't know if that's what they call it….but I could tell it was lotion with sand and rocks in it and she is rubbing it all over my face. Just imagine going to the beach….ok…now your face is a little wet… and then the wind blows a bunch of sand on your face……ok now put some suntan lotion on and start rubbing it in…..**OH YEA**…. facial scrub at its finest…….**dead skin…be gone!!!** So after the sanding of the skin she asks me…..I think she asked me….or maybe

Jane told her to do it as a surprise….**about…a facial peel…**I can't remember. I say tell me about it, because at this point I am totally relaxed I really mean it I'm totally relaxed….so she starts to tell me about the peel….she describes it as.. a lot of dead skin has layered up on my face and we need to peel it off……**I think what the heck**…..after hearing all the benefits…how could I not get it done? All of a sudden she starts applying this stuff…..**(ACID)** and my face feels like **it's on fire**….not like a regular fire…..**I mean a 5 alarm fire…..an out of control fire….bubbling skin fire….I'm feeling like maybe it's going to "burn all the skin off my face" fire!!!!** She tells me to relax that this isn't the stuff that really hurts…this is just the prep stuff to get your face ready…..well I tell her to forget the real stuff…this is killing me!!! She is looking at me like **I'm some kind of a wimp….I am….**I admit it….but I have to tell ya….this was the craziest thing I've done in my lifetime….well maybe not my lifetime, but in quite a while. So I tell her to go ahead with the rest of the peel and now it is a 5 alarm fire and I'm thinking that if I don't die at least all my wrinkles will be gone. OK it's the next day and **my face is feeling a little tight…..**and my wrinkles seem to have gotten worse…if that's possible….my wife tells me it's ok….you will start to peel.. and it will soften up in a few days. I wake up the next day and it's true……**I'm looking like a snake losing its skin….**I'm peeling all over my face…and where the dead skin has fallen off….the skin underneath is smooth as a baby's butt and a different color. My goal was to make me look younger…..**like that's possible!!!!** Well I have to tell you….after a few days and with the memory of the **facial fire** faded in the distance…I found myself wanting more….so I will be going back in a week or so to get some more.. I will keep you up to date on how my face is or isn't doing….

WHOOPS, I DID IT AGAIN!

I think I'll update you all on some of the stuff that has been written about and then dropped for a while. First let me begin with "WHOOPS I DID IT AGAIN!" No not that Brittany Spears and I are getting married.....It's highly unlikely that I would marry someone so young and busy!...I'm talking about my re-entry into the stock world. OK....now think back to last year when I invested a few bucks on a tip from my son Ben...yeh.. you remember...the stock was the famous "XOXO" and the other was Nextel....well I bought 500 shares of **XOXO** and not Nextel. Well about 3 hours after I bought the **XOXO** stock.. the company went bankrupt. The stock price of Nextel was at about $2.50 a share... which I didn't buy....now it's about $28.00 a share....which would only be a $12,500 to $25,000 profit...who knew?.....Not Me!!!! Well about 2 weeks ago I bought quite a few shares of Sun Micro Systems at a good price.....thinking I could make a few easy bucks....in no time at all...so I could pay off some taxes...well the first week I was living the day trader's dream....my money was working for me.... and just when every stock was climbing.... my stock seemed to hit a bump in the road. Within a few days.... everything I gained was gone and my money was now losing money...within a few days I had lost hundreds of bucks......quickly I panicked....as it seemed to me that the stock market was about to crash......I pulled my money out....licked my wounds and carried on.....the day I pulled my money out....YUP...the stock started to rise.....within a few days if my money would have still been in I would have gained a bunch....I invested in Martha Stewart the day she was getting out of jail with thoughts of making a bundle. The only bundle I made was learning how to fold a bundle of towels by watching her TV show.

I lost a bunch and went into panic mode and pulled again. Well so much for me and the market...Next time I'll just burn the money when I think of it!!

GOING ONCE, GOING TWICE

OK here we go again….I know that some of you probably think I sit around and make these stories up. Well I don't and I'm kinda glad this stuff happens to me and Jane, because I wouldn't have anything to write about if it didn't. OK it starts out in Benicia where we are going to attend an auction at the Clocktower…..I usually will end up buying something…usually it's the toilet paper from Hayes Janitorial…the box lasts about a year. Well this night I was feeling like something special was about to happen…..and it did…The auctioneer was making me crazy and all of a sudden nothing mattered or made any sense. I found myself going for an auction item just to go for it….yea you got it….I was trying to out- bid a friend named Lory who works with me and I was determined not to lose. I was totally out of my mind….I don't drink and it felt like I was drunk…all I could think of was (I really need this) and I really didn't….It was air fare round trip to Las Vegas with 2 nights stay at the Bellagio Hotel and a concert to see Celine Dion with great seats. Well the auctioneer was really working us against each other….at one point he said "and I'll throw in a red carpet dinner at Benihana's with the owner….how could I pass this up? I couldn't….so my paddle kept going up….way after what would have been a reasonable price….I was still bidding…Someone should have slapped me…maybe I would have woke up from this crazy dream… Next thing I know I won the trip and I looked around the room and Lory looked over at me like she was just trying to make me pay!!!! She did it…she got me to pay way more that I should have…..So how I justified it was…we really wanted to see Celine and the money was for a good cause…..the real reason was….I just got caught up in the moment….OK it's about 3 days before we are heading down to Vegas to see Celine and guess what....YOU guessed it..... she canceled her concert dates for a while and we were out of luck...we still had the hotel booked and couldn't get the money back so we told the people we would stay one extra night...and that added new air fare of $260...on me....Oh My! Well the whole idea of the mini vacation was to go to the concert...so now were stuck for the MAJOR bucks just to stay in Vegas for 3 days to wander around the casino and spend more money.....I kinda felt like I had been had....Actually the best thing about the trip was the free dinner at Benihana's...yup they knew we were coming and Roly made sure we were taken care of....That was the best $2,000 dinner we ever flew to. I had never stayed at the Bellagio before....I was quite impressed.....I was blown away at the cost....I thought the price was for the whole time we would be there and it was just for one of the nights....In the room there was a folder that had everything in the room for sale...yup you can buy anything in the room even the mattresses....for a mere $1,600 you can have the mattress you slept on....there is even a mirror in the bathroom that lights up and magnifies your face for $390. I'll take it! Did I mention that cokes were only $4....what a deal...Ya know we did have a good time relaxing by the pool....all day long....at one point I fell asleep for about an hour, and when I woke up I thought we were in the silicon valley....wait a minute...we were in the silicon valley.....totally unbelievable....it just had nothing to do with computers. When I was laying there by the pool a thought came to me......I could be laying at a pool anywhere and I would have felt just fine.....so why was I at a place that for 3 nights 20 years ago I could have bought a car? OH that's right I won this at an auction...Next time you see me at an auction in Benicia or anywhere else for that matter..... help me....let me know you read the story and you are there to let me know it's OK to be out-bid for something you really didn't want in the first place. You know the only thing I can say about the whole thing is I got the booby prize...yup that's what you get when you go sit by the pool at the Bellagio for three days....You get the booby prize....Just a small note about the gym at the hotel....Great gym…lots of machines…free bottled water…yup $3.50 in the room and free in the gym…they had flat screen T.V.s at the front of every machine…headphones and T.V. I was in Heaven….worked out on a machine pretty similar to the one I use at my gym in town….There must have been something very different with the machines at the Hotel….the next day I couldn't bend my legs…they hurt so bad…. it felt like someone had punched them a bunch of times….trying to get back a couple of the free bottles of water…I was not going to give them up!

A PILATES LIFE FOR ME

I have a new theory about birthdays...**Next month I will be 54**....now some of you are reading this and saying..."that's still very young" and some of you are saying...."Wow he's really old". I still feel like about 30 to 35 so I have come up with a new way to count...and enjoy my birthdays a whole lot more. Instead of turning 54 **next month I'm going to turn 52**....Yea you got it right...I'm going to go backwards from this year on. Just think about it.... maybe I will catch up to how I'm feeling...this could change the way we age! In just 3 years from now I'll be 49...and even though that still is way, way older than I feel and think....at least it's a step in the right direction. Just think.....in 13 years I'll be 39 instead of 67....now I ask you...which one do you want to be?

OK here is another month of fun and torture! When you read this I will just be turning 52.....It's my first birthday going backwards....I am looking so forward to getting younger!!!! For those of you who are reading this for the first time or if you missed a few months back....I have decided to turn back time.....instead of me going to be 54...I will actually go backwards and get some of the time I have missed...It's a real good feeling to think I will be in my 40's in the next few years! OK let's get on to some of the stuff I have been doing to actually stay young and fit...You know I have been going to the gym now for a year and 3 months....If you've seen me you probably are thinking.....What's he doing at the gym...he doesn't look very buffed and what are those love handles doing there still after all this time? I have to tell you....I have been working my self to death....I go to the gym at least 3 or 4 times a week and sometimes more. When I first started going it was easy because I was eating right and the weight was dropping right off me...a lot of hard work, but my weight was just saying bye bye...well after about a year of the same old routine...I started to crave some of the things from my (fat) past. I still am sticking to the no hamburgers or pizza, but as for ice cream, candy and donuts, and chips and salsa at Randy's.......well I have broken down, but I'm not gaining any weight....well I have gained back about 10 pounds, but every week I tell myself I'm going to lose it next week.....So what happens is if I eat to much.... I have to spend more time at the gym...so lately I have been at the gym about 5 and 6 days a week....Killing myself....If I could just stop the input....I could slow down on the output.....NOOOO not me...that would be to easy...I just got an MP3 player....High tech for me but I got it down now....I down load all my favorite tunes and use the machine that best describes my workout routine...the ep-i-lep-tic machine...the one where your hands are doing one thing and your feet are doing another and every 5 minutes it starts to go backwards....I just hold on for dear life....the music is the only thing that keeps me on the machine...otherwise....I quit...every now and then my battery goes dead in my MP3 when I'm on the machine.... I immediately get off and do something else. (No music...No workout) So I was thinking maybe I can do something else to rip my body into shape...that would be a little less taxing....When I walk into the gym I always see a group of girls doing this crazy stuff they call Pilates Reformer Training....looks pretty easy to me...and hey it's a bunch of women....how hard could it be? I signed up for my first class....I see all the stars on T.V. doing Pilates and they look in pretty good shape....probably cause that's all they have to do... besides tell their cooks what great healthy meal they would like for dinner. So I show up for my class....9:30 in the morning and I'm feeling pretty good....4 women & the instructor (Female) (Jane) no relation. The machine right away looked a little intimidating, but you have got to remember I have been working out for a while now. The class starts and I'm feeling pretty good...a lot of stretching and a lot of breathing....yup you have got to remember to breath...now I know that sounds like no big deal, but I found myself pushing and pulling and forgetting to breath. There is a whole lot to just pulling and pushing and crossing and bending and sweating and sweating and sweating and bending and pushing and squeezing...the girls are making it look really easy and I don't want to look bad, so I pretend like I have it handled and it's no big deal....I'm actually killing myself....but I'm smiling the whole time in case one of the women is looking....trying to make myself look good and strong. The whole class is an hour long and man do you go through some strange and vigorous exercise..Still smiling (and dying) and every now and then getting complemented by my teacher...I was feeling pretty darn good...All right finally the class was over and I was soaking wet to say the least....I walked out of the class waving goodbye to the ladies feeling like I had just been jumped by a gang and beat up real bad. I ran off at the mouth like I could do this everyday....no problem....the only problem was trying to get out of bed the next morning...Oh my God I felt like I was paralyzed and finally after getting up the only problem was walking...the day was challenging to say the least and the next day was worse...I guess I hadn't worked those muscles before....like never in the past 53 years. It felt like someone had a tight hold of my butt cheeks and weren't going to let them go and kept squeezing tighter and tighter with every step.... It also felt like someone had put 50 pound weights on my calves...I was a beat down man....This was quite the reality check I needed.... this was no girlie workout...this was for those people who are out of their minds and real serious about torture and getting fit....You know in a very, very sick kind of way I want to go back. Girls rule Boys Drool!

I BROKE YOUR BRAKE

Wow....It's already Summer......I can't believe it! I hope this summer I can write some exciting stories about us going to some fun places where nothing happens to me except sun and fun.....Yea like that's going to happen.... the chances of an ordinary summer without daily natural disasters happening...are slim to none! Pretty soon towns will probably pay me for not showing up! Well here we go....Last month my buddy Phil had a birthday and he asked us if we wanted to go out to San Francisco to dinner....most of the time when we go out somewhere he always wants to go out after dinner and go to go to a blues club. Now...I love the blues and I used to love to go anywhere to listen to music.....I think something has happened to the exciting side of my life...you know the adventure side...the....yea let's go do it side! All I can think of now when he suggests it is.....Oh no...loud music...smoke...people....late night....long drive...drunks...you get it...as I think about this I cringe, because this is what I lived for...it was always **all or nothing.**...I'm getting old and don't want to admit it! Do you feel like I do? OK...It's on...Phil calls and we meet at his house...because we have the biggest car....I get to drive....yup...S.F. This is another thing I think that has worn itself out...in the getting excited to go somewhere department. Driving... in S.F..... people don't drive...they merge...whenever they feel like it! A couple of weeks ago I was in the City and a cab driver started yelling at me to drive better....can you imagine that....I couldn't get over it....I started yelling back at him telling him...If he kept it up I wouldn't come back to the City anymore. I really did....every stop light I took the liberty to yell back at him.....It felt pretty good! OK so we head over to the City and we get a little lost...in real heavy traffic…up the hills and down the hills….you know the ones….when you are going down….all you can think about is…what would happen if my brakes gave out? And up those hills where all you can think about is….I hope my car doesn't stall…The one thing that makes everything all good is **a horn**….everybody's honking…. They must be trying to get my attention to say hi, because they all honk at me! I just keep waving and smiling…. **OK**..So we finally find the restaurant and pull right up to the front door….because as you know there is no parking within a mile or so of anything you want to do. I see a valet parking sign….and it's only $15…you got it Only $15. Think about it….park a mile away and maybe you make it to the restaurant and maybe you don't..I'll pay the fifteen bucks. So we go in and this is a fine restaurant….very elegant hotel and Italian dinner house. This is supposed to be the best it gets in San Francisco, but we get there a little early and they are great to us and let us have a table. We settle in and order some appetizers……A little time goes by and we have been eating bread and stuff at the table and then one of the waiters comes to our table and asks if I'm the one with the gold Tahoe….I say yes….All I can think is that someone has come down the hill and smashed into it….and he says……How do you get the brake off? And I tell him to pull on the handle that has **the word brake** on it. He goes off and comes back to the table about 10 minutes later….Once again he says sir how do you get the parking brake off? Again I tell him….just pull the lever marked parking brake….So…I get up and go out to the car to give them some help….I look at the emergency foot brake pedal and he has pushed it so far down that it has become part of the floorboard with a little carpet puffed around it…I lift the handle to release the brake and it's broken….I get out of the car…lean down…look under the dash and see that he has **snapped my brake cable** and the emergency brake is not coming undone….As it looks like this is a time when I would normally scream at someone I don't; I'm so mad, but I keep my cool….I start pacing, because it's a lot better than fighting….They make it seem like it could have been my fault….I'm old and don't fight very good anymore….and I really didn't want to see if I could whip the manager lady who seemed kind of concerned anyway! I pulled the lever up that releases the brake and they have stuck the wires back in the hole to make it look like when I pulled it I broke it and that pissed me off. Phil comes out to the rescue and kind of undoes the brake pedal and the car will move but we have to drive home with the bell ringing all the way. Annoyed and taken aback that the manager of the restaurant didn't offer to pay to have it fixed or comp our meal....I am going to have to get a new brake cable put in, but I can't find the time to leave my car for a day...I feel like letting you know the name of the restaurant, but I'm going to let them decide what to do with the bill...either way I will let you know...Good Restaurant....Or Baaaaadddddd Restaurant....we went back in and had a great meal and enjoyed ourselves. The ride home was nerve racking to say the least...as the bell went off every 5 seconds all the way home. I gotta get this fixed quick or bust the bell. The parking, the new brake, the meal, the gas and everything about the evening ran about $200.00, but I can say it was kind of worth it......

End of Broke my Brake

You know this last couple of months have just flown by and a lot has happened. I never heard from the restaurant in San Francisco where my brake was broke...You know I have to be honest with you all...The restaurant is a great place to eat and have your car parked, but I just have that cloud that sometimes hangs over me that I can't avoid. Yes they did break the brake, but I would still eat there. I must admit...I have made some mistakes in my life....and they made a mistake...I am going to forgive them...so if you are in the S.F. area and want to pick up a great Italian Meal..... go to an Italian restaurant. If they would have responded I would have given you their name, but they never responded to my letter or my bill, but maybe they were busy. Baddddddddddd Businessssssssssssssss.

THONGS FOR THE MEMORIES

A lot of people have seemed surprised to see me this month. I don't know if they thought I was still in the hospital or just checked out for good! I got out of the hospital doing great....all I needed was a little R & R so we went to Hawaii. Boy I tell ya I sure have been going through it...I remember back to '68.. yea that's when I graduated...what a great year. I feel like it was just yesterday or maybe the day before....well it's been 35 years...where did they go? It kinda feels like someone tricked me and took away about 25 of them without telling me. I mean...don't get me wrong I had a blast......I think I did anyway. Ya know it just seemed to hit me about a year ago that my hair had turned grey, and I had a lot more forehead. I remember the long dark ponytail, and the white...snakeskin boots....heck I remember the bell-bottoms, and the guru shirts....I remember floaters....they were shoes that floated...what for I still don't know! I remember being a Greaser...a Surfer and then a Hippie....I even went through an all white gauss period where I thought I was a guru...I even went through a period where I thought I was a rocker...I couldn't play anything...but the role itself!! Man I remember the Avalon Ballroom, The Fillmore, Monterey Pop Festival, Haight Ashbury, Peoples Park in Berkeley. They say if you remember the 60's you weren't there.....I was there.... I don't remember much , but I remember I was there. I remember the 70's and I remember the Bee Gee's and Donna Summers and disco dancing....I was a good dancer...I think....You know I've had quite the life...and I know I shouldn't complain, but....this getting old stuff is starting to get to me....It would be different if I felt 53, but I don't.........I feel 30 or 31 or 32 or 33 or somewhere around that age...maybe I am.....maybe they messed up on my delivery date....you never know....Maybe someone has been playing tricks on me and dying my hair grey when I'm asleep.....Maybe I did miss the 60's. Well as you can see.........I really have been going through it..... I've been talking about a face lift, hair transplants, a man-boob reduction, dying my hair jet black like Roy Orbison...a tuck here and a tuck there....and then I think to myself....hey you are who you are and it took a lot of time and fun times to get you here...and I get happy for a minute....and then I think........What if I did all that stuff and nobody recognized me anymore...heck what if I didn't recognize myself. OK I won't do anything crazy to my body...wait a minute...when I was in Hawaii I couldn't wait to get a tattoo...didn't get one cause you had to not go in the sun or in the water....go figure....I was in Hawaii....(no tattoo) So if you see me on main street with dark hair...and I start to take on the Elvis look...just humor me and tell me "it looks great and very natural" You know I feel good just letting the cat out of the bag....maybe we all go through this...I mean the people over 40 or so....it seems like everyone I ask how old they are...they always say "but I feel 20 years younger". I am going to end this for now, but if you do see me.... really I mean it...humor me...with something like "hey what have you been doing...you look like you are getting younger everyday" I will know you are lying, but what the heck....it will probably make me feel good! OK let's go to Hawaii for a minute.....Palm trees, beautiful beaches, hot sand, thongs....did I say thongs? I don't mean the kind you wear on your feet...I mean the bathing suits....are they hiding all the girls that wear them? I was at the beach for an entire week and I saw one....and maybe she didn't really know what it looked like from behind. After seeing her I want to blank the whole trip out of my mind. I do know one thing...we have gotten a bit heavy...yea I mean all of us...boy that image of Baywatch babes on the beach we see on TV and in the movies is really not reality...I really didn't feel like I was on the set of Bay Watch while I was there this time. I'm talking about men and women and myself included, I decided that we are what we are...and we love food and life and so what if we are a little or a whole lot heavy.....seems as though it is in fashion in Hawaii....at first I was thinking...how could they? Then after a few days on the beach....you realize..........what the heck! God gave us these beautiful bodies and instead of covering them up....let it all hang out...you aren't going to see the people you saw on vacation ever again...so get comfortable with it!! I am planning a trip back to the islands in January and I'm buying a thong...you got it...let's give them something to talk about when they get back to Kansas or wherever they are from. C-Ya

WING DING

It's September and there are Decorations........You gotta be kidding me! Christmas decorations will be all over the stores in a few days. Did I miss it or didn't we have a summer? I'm sure this was not only the fastest summer ever, but also the coolest and I don't mean COOL as in COOL...It seemed like a 70's Summer............Not disco cool.........Cool like the 70's.... a lot of long pants days....I'm not a real pants guy....I mean I like wearing pants just not long ones....Shorts....are my thing...kinda like these stories....short stories. Thank god they are short stories or nobody would read them. Now that I've confused you let's get on with the month.....I finally got the hospital to give me an MRI on my hip.....Yup....I've been dragging my leg and complaining for the last two years about my hip and they have just kind of let it go.....I've been given a few different prescriptions to ward off the pain and a few of the miracle drugs to mask the pain....and finally they listened to me....so I got the MRI..... and they tell me that there is a 1 inch sist on the ball of my hip...Sist....or is it...cist.... or cyst..who cares how to spell it....what is it? When can you get it out of my body? I just don't seem to be anyone's emergency at the hospital unless I'm holding my chest and breathing hard....they finally scheduled me an appointment...So I head to the hospital and check in and I'm stripped down to my shorts in the ice cold room....laying on the table...and the doc comes in and seems really confused and asks me...why are you seeing me today? I'm thinking how to make my answer in the form of a question, because I must be on Jeopardy. He says there is no reason for you to be here, as you are scheduled to have an MRI on Thursday.....I'm confused.... I tell him...I don't know what's going on...you folks scheduled it....

maybe for the co-pay....just figure a few thousand mistakes like that a day....could buy a new wing for the hospital in a few years.......
The Doc calls a few days after the MRI and says to come in and see him....I tell him I have called and scheduled an appointment in a few days.... and he tells me...let me make sure you are scheduled to come in....and he says...OK...So I show up....with Jane...I go to the window and the lady says.....You don't have an appointment today...who scheduled you? I tell her my doctor...and she tells me to come back on Sept. 2nd. I'm an easy going guy....so I start to leave...Jane is not so easy going today, so she says....hey we want to see the doctor today...the lady at the window is not as sweet as you would imagine someone who is suppose to be nice. I just feel like if you are always a bummer....someone should fire your ass. So the lady writes a little note for the doc to have him talk to me in-between appointments....and a few minutes later out comes his secretary...who looks confused and says the doctor never talked to me and it was the nurse who scheduled the appointment for the 2nd..........I say no....the person had a very deep voice and called himself Dr..... and she totally disputes what I had heard. I know it's not me I'm a really nice guy and never bring my bad day into any ones life. Her attitude is as bad as the lady at the window.... maybe they live together and had a fight this morning. Confused and still hurting...we leave, but not before stopping at the window to see our other best friend in the lobby....Jane asks....what if it's a cancerous cyst...what should we do then? The sweet lady at the desk looks up and says....as in the form of a question...another Jeopardy question....would you have to go to a cancer clinic? I don't know why we are asking her......Oh never mind...I'm sure if it was cancer they would have gotten a hold of me before the end of the year. I'll be back soon to pay another co-pay. Maybe with all these extra co-pays they will name a wing after me....I doubt it....but if they do.... I would like it to be called Wing Ding!

NEWSWEEK MAGAZINE

You should have come to Hawaii with Jane and I...we had a blast and we really missed you! Some great stuff happened to us while we were there....Like we both ended up in the hospital one morning...yea...check this out....we went to Napili beach in Maui one afternoon when the waves were crashing on the beach pretty hard and they really were much bigger than normal...Jane and I, our daughter Jodie and her husband Rick were all pretending to be body surfing....I say pretending, because body surfing is out in the ocean and we were standing on the sand waiting for the waves to come slam us against the sand and hurl us head over heals up the sandy beach. We were watching all the little kids do it and it seemed like fun......At one point the waves were coming in really fast and huge....While I was waiting for the next wave I noticed Jane being slammed into the sand and dragged up the beach almost to the where people were sitting....although I was deeply concerned for her safety I couldn't stop laughing uncontrollably. Now she is flipping over and being dragged down towards the waves again when...Yup another wave slams her down and up the beach again.....I know it's mean, but I was laughing harder than ever now....and so is everyone on the beach...all of a sudden I see Jodie get caught up in the wave and is being tossed and rolled up the beach. I noticed some local surfer boys who also were enjoying what was happening, as Jodie was rolling up the beach her top was up and bottom down and the boys were happy. All of a sudden we were grabbed by a huge wave and....SLAMMED against the sand....up the beach to the top.....rolling, spinning, flipping, losing our bathing suits, because they were so full of sand...each time we stood up it looked like we had a big load in the pants....Now Rick is in the picture….we were having a blast…and so was everyone on the beach….I'm not sure if it was because our suits were coming off or they were thinking…."are these people crazy?" All in all it was pretty fun….the night before I slept kinda crazy and my neck had got a kink in it. Now the waves and the slamming had readjusted most of my muscle groups and bones I was feeling like someone had ripped off my head…and I could no longer move it…When we woke up the next morning I couldn't move my head and Jane couldn't hear, because there was too much sand and water in her ears. We called Kaiser and headed off to the hospital…when we went in I noticed that we were the only Mainlanders…yup all locals…looking at us like….DAHH tourists! Well we got to see the doctors and they gave me valium and drained Jane's ears…I could move my head a little and Jane could hear again, I had lost the enthusiasm to be in Hawaii as soon as the valium hit….all I wanted to do was sleep…. but my neck felt better and now I could turn my head around to see what was going on around me. Call us stupid, but the slamming into the beach and the acting like little kids wasn't out of us yet….. YEA you guessed it….back to the beach…Slamming, laughing, flipping, losing the suits…eating tons of sand….and now the valium made the slams even more fun…they didn't hurt as much……what a great day in paradise! One day we went looking for a really great place to bogey board…everyone told us to go to Big Beach on the other side of the island…long drive…got there….Glass…not a wave in sight..only old folks…including ourselves! Yup all the waves were in Napali…We had driven to Big Beach and we stopped by a fish taco truck on the way back…..Oh my….Called Jaws 2…the best tacos….to die for…when we pulled up there was just us and by the time we had eaten our tacos there were people everywhere. The taco truck also sold shaved ice and Jane wanted a shaved ice and I looked at the line…about 20 deep…went to the side door and Jane yelled into the truck if she could order there…he said no…I said hey man I loved he tacos…. and I told him I was going to do a story about the Taco truck…he asked me "who I wrote for" without thinking and because the pressure was on with my wife…. I said

Newsweek...(a little lie)....this guy was all mine and he wanted to tell me everything about his life. He made sure Jane got her Shaved Ice...You know sometimes you gotta do what you gotta do....for your wife!...It really was a News—Week!

WHAT HEART ATTACK?

On to the Hip business....I sit here typing in pain after my surgery...they went in the side of my leg and drilled up into the ball of the hip and removed a cyst. OUCH OUCH OUCH....well something really weird happened when I went to see the doctor....he tells me they can't put me under because of the problems I've had with my heart. I tell him I'm feeling pretty good these days and he says "after last year's heart attack we have to be careful." WHAT did you say....Heart attack? I didn't have a heart attack. He says oh yes you did it says it right here in your file. I tell him again....no I didn't have a heart attack...you must have the files mixed up....I'm Earl Miller...He says Yup.....were you in the hospital last year for some chest pains? and I say yes and he says..... well that was a heart attack....I am totally blown away....maybe they should have told me then...maybe I would have eaten different, and maybe a few more push-ups, and no bacon or pizza.....I don't know what to say at this point except....OK. So I tell the doctor if they are only going to put the bottom half asleep...what's going to happen to the top? He tells me that they are going to sedate me...and I'm not happy....I don't want to hear the drill and smell the burning bone as they drill up into my hip. He assures me I'll be sedated, but I'm still kinda scared....you could say I'm kind of a big baby when it comes to people drilling into me. Well I remembered talking to the doctor just before the operation and I told him to make sure I was sedated.......I was...I woke up and I was in the recovery room..... Heavily Sedated.... I couldn't feel anything! I do mean anything.... for hours...I thought I would never walk again......Well I am happy to tell you I am walking with the help of the crutches....and that's a story in itself....crutches....oh what a joy! The best part about the crutches was going to the SF airport and being shuttled from the curb to the seat of the plane in a wheelchair. When I got to Boston they were right there and ready to pick me up...I got to tell you about the guy who sat next to me in the plane....I think it was the guy that was made famous for singing She Bangs She Bangs...After we take off from SF airport there is a seat between me and this other guy....he decides to get some sleep and leans over and lays his head on my leg.......REALLY....I flip out and tell him that I just had an operation and I'm really sore and could he not lean on me. He says OK and puts his head on the seat next to me and kind of pins me between him and the arm of my chair with his head. I can't believe it...this can't be happening to me...he lifts his legs up on the wall above the windows and is kinda pushing me...I try to tell him that he has got to stop it, but he's asleep. I call for a flight attendant and ask it there are any other places I can sit and they say we're all full up. All of a sudden when I was talking to the lady he yells out Water...Water...Like get me some...no please or anything.... just.....Water...the lady brings him the water and he doesn't get up...he lays on his side drinking it and making a lot of noise sipping it from the side of the cup. I'm still pinned into my seat and his head against me. I kinda doze off for a few minutes and all of a sudden this guy is crushing his plastic cup and making all kind of noise with the cup....He was trying to get the attention of the attendant....I am fully awake now and I can't take it any longer..... I yell into his face from about 2 inches away...which is right at my leg..... **YOOOOOOOOO! Cut it out.** He looks at me and looks annoyed, but he does stop crushing the cup and I grab it from him and he just closes his eyes and dozes off. Just before we land he gets out his phone and makes a phone call and unbuckles his seat belt...at this time I want to hurt him. When we stop he starts to push me out of the way to get to his bags...I let him go by...Or else I would have killed him. How do I always seem to get the weirdest people on the planet?

THROW AWAY THE CRUTCHES

L et's address the Hip thing...Got new crutches to go to Mexico with me for my first hip operation and used them quite a bit, but I'm still feeling too much pain to think about it! Flew into Mexico on vacation...yea I know.... I do go on a lot of vacations....My brother in-law Steve set it up without us knowing anything about where we were going......Just told us we were going to have a great time in a real nice place...I had dreams of room service, swim up bars (for my Pepsi) big flat screen TV, and a real nice rent-a-car......NOPE....We ended up in a town with dirt streets and ladies cooking chickens on make-shift grills at the corners. No room service...no fancy restaurants...no fancy rent-a-car...we had to rent a jeep, why....I'll tell you why....because the road to the place we rented was up a hill of river rocks...and there was no other way to get up there. It was completely impossible to get there on crutches. The first night we stayed there was a spider in our room the size of a small dog and he was walking all over the walls and believe it or not a crab...not a little crab...a big crab...and we were about a half mile from the water....I still can't figure that one out. I scooted the crab out of my room with a broom, because I didn't want to kill it...Jane's mom and dad were staying downstairs from us and in the morning they told us that there was a crab in their room last night and they smashed it!! I just laughed knowing I swept the crab into their direction. I killed the spider that was in our room that night and the next day I told someone in town and they said it was a scorpion eating spider and they are harmless (Huge but harmless) made me feel a little insecure about what might be lurking around my room the next night and made it almost impossible to get to sleep. The next day I thought I needed a break away from my crutches…So I rented a surf board…crutched out to the water dropped the crutches and got out in the surf….80 degree water and life was all it could be for about 15 minutes and then I caught a wave….jumped up to my knees and my hip and leg felt like they had been ripped off my body…the most intense pain you could imagine….I just cried and stayed put on my knees until I hit the sand and the board came to a screeching halt….then I rolled and fell forward over the end of the board and crawled on my knees to my crutches and left the surfing for the younger crowd. Left Mexico and guess what I got to bring back over the boarder? No duty free booze or perfume just Montezuma's Revenge…yes as bad as it could get…it makes it hard to do anything….even getting up makes you weak…it felt like someone pushed a rat inside my stomach and it was trying to eat its way out….

FART ATTACK

I got home from Mexico with the Revenge in full-on mode and I had to go to the east coast the next day.....I took the red eye and I was flying first class and I needed an aisle seat...so I got on the plane first (because of the crutches) and sat in the aisle seat and some young guy comes up and says "that's my seat.... and I tell him that I'm not feeling so good and I will be using the bathroom quite a bit....he says...please let me have my seat! I tell him once more that I have brought back the revenge from Mexico and he ignores me. So I move over and he immediately falls asleep....every time I have to go to the bathroom I have to jump over his legs.....in the condition I was in....that wasn't really the best thing for me to be doing. I could have smacked him, but I got back at him....I had a case of the worse GAS you could ever imagine....I couldn't get up every time I needed to fart so when I had to fart I acted like I was asleep and hoped the attendants thought it was the guy next to me....Oh my god it smelled terrible and oh what a miserable night...One I will never forget...You probably won't either!! While I was gone back east the election happened....this is the first time I didn't get to vote...I felt really bad....I was in New Hampshire and there were people everywhere with Kerry signs....I do mean everywhere....the day after the election the whole state was depressed....A very dark day....I'm sure glad he didn't lose or win by one vote! It could have only happened to me. Jane and I took a ride around the east coast one day while we were back there and it started to get dark, so we headed towards the hotel. I really have never got used to the highways back there, but I knew my way back to where we were staying....(I thought) after driving about an hour....we were lost...very lost.... it seemed like we drove through every small town in the state of

New Hampshire….I knew we were headed in the right direction…..
until we came upon a sign…..Welcome to Maine! Oh No….all the
time we were on the road I thought we were going West….Nope
we were heading East…..all the way….we finally got home….late…
late…late that night…I wanted to tell you about the rent a car place
I had the pleasure of working with in the Boston area when we got
there….It was cheap and bizarre….and Yes I saved money, but what
a weird, weird experience. First off…they were not situated near the
airport….as I recall I got in a bus and for a moment I was under the
impression I was being kidnapped….I really mean it….When I got
there…**the lady said they were out of the car I had paid for** and
they would have to charge me 50 dollars more…you would think
that if they were out of the car I had asked for and reserved and paid
for in advance they should give me a discount, as I wasn't renting an
economy car I always rent a big car. It was not my day and I didn't
want to have them drive me back to the airport so I paid the lady.
Everything from leaving Mexico was all downhill!!! C-Ya

PUSHIN' TOO HARD

Happy New Year to You all!!.....Hey folks it's a new year and usually I go over all the things that have happened to me over the year past....Not this year...It seems as though all the things that have happened are still happening. You are probably wondering...or maybe you are as sick of the hip story as I am...Well here is an up date...I went to the hospital to get a shot right in the hip ball to make it stop hurting....I hate shots...I don't know if you are like me, but I can't stand the thought of getting a shot...I always look the other way and think that the needle is going to break off in me. Maybe I'm just a paranoid...I guess I am a paranoid. Well I get into the office and the doctor tells me to drop My drawers and I do. Then I get on the table and cover my eyes....I know I sound like a big baby, but did you listen to me when I said he was going to put the needle in my hip ball? Do you know how far the hip ball is in from the outer layer of your skin...I have some big ole legs! The needle looked as though it could have been a foot long, I know it wasn't but it sure seemed like it! So first he puts some Novocain in the area that is going to be punctured. So he starts guiding the needle in....further and further....deeper and deeper...I can hear it going through the skin...It is making me sick....I start making a little noise so I can't hear it. I know he has it all the way in because his hand is pressing real hard against my skin....He pulls out the needle and he say's we have to try another needle, because this one is too short.....Too short...I can't believe it...I thought it would have gone all the way through my leg. So he says he's going to go down the hall and find a longer needle....I'm freaked out at this point...I felt like I should be compensated for the mishap...like a hundred bucks or something...like maybe I could give the doctor a shot....one that's too short...like in his neck!! He comes back in the room....I can't see the new needle, but I know it's the size of a turkey baster....all I can do is turn my head and cringe...He starts the new needle in the leg and this time is driving it in at a slower pace to make sure he gets it in the right place. You are not going to believe this....The second needle was to short, or he just missed the hip bone completely.......I know he was going to want to give it one more try so I jumped off the bed and pulled up my pants and said....You know I don't feel any pain anymore....I believe I have been cured....He just laughs and tells me he will schedule me an appointment to have me come into the x-ray dept. and we will guide the needle into the exact area that it needs to go....I'm thinking.... what's this guy....nuts? Like I'm going to come back for more of this!!! Not in this lifetime...So the next week there I am back at the hospital...and only because of the extreme pain...Off to the x-ray room...get this...I get to lay on the table and watch the needle go in to my hip on a big screen above my face...I have to be honest.... this time it didn't hurt as bad as the first time...It could have had something to do with the muscle relaxer I took right before I went in....I didn't tell him...I just acted brave. We took a walk after I got the shot...of Novocain and cortisone and I felt like the old me within the hour....Then I went home and got up the next day and felt like the old me...Yea the OLD me...the shot didn't work...I was back in the pain zone....Guess what....I'm going back and we are going to have to do something new!! I will keep you up to date. Yesterday I was in Fairfield and a lady was kind of staring at me.... I thought maybe she either she knew me or my zipper was down.... then she said...aren't you Cookin with Earl? I said yes...what else could I do...I wondered if she ever read these weird stories, but I didn't ask. Then I went to the Macy's at the mall about a half an hour later and a lady at the watch counter said...aren't you the real estate guy in Benicia...I said yes...what else could I have said? No I'm Cookin with Earl. No I'm the guy who writes the stories from the Big Chair. No I'm the guy who runs the program for the kids. What I have come to realize is that I love doing what I do...

everything I do! I want to thank all of you for putting up with me over all these years...Let's make this the best year ever....Let's live some of our dreams...Let's go the extra mile...Let's help those in need...Let's love our children even more. Let's always remember to tell those around you how much they mean to you and how much you really love them.....Mom....I miss you I wish you were still here and thank you for my life!

DON'T BUG ME

Hey we just flew in from Mexico and I have quite a few stories…..so let me clue you in on just a few…First let me tell you a little about where we were. North of Puerto Vallarta in a very small village with some very large bugs…The village is located in the middle of a rain forest 60 miles wide and 120 miles long. If you stop to think about it for a minute…think about all the movies you have seen about the rain forest……Bugs and snakes and BIG…I MEAN BIG…….I mean large!…Each morning when I got up to get my coffee I would sweep the tiles first thing or step on quite a few bugs. I kept the broom right next to my bedroom door. A lot of little bugs, but lots of big ones too…Crabs too! Yea crabs…land crabs. Well one day I was minding my own business and I look up into the sky and all of a sudden it got dark and this thing is coming towards me and it sounds like a small plane….It's dark and big and looks like someone threw their cell phone at me….nope….It's a flying Beetle….yup a flying beetle… the size of a cell phone…not.. no little phone…not no little razor phone…..this was a huge Beetle….it looked out of control when it flew by my head and then landed, but when it landed it landed on its back. When I ran over to it, it was spinning around trying to get over on its belly and long swing blade looking legs. It was weird…It would get its sharp end of the tip of its leg on some grout between the tile and get a grip and push off and spin like a top……I thought it was going to flip over and get me. I really didn't know what to do except panic….I was going to stomp on it with my flip flops, but I thought it was so big it would be a lot of blood and I could see it going all over my legs. I'm not even sure these things have blood, but the thought of stomping on it made me sick to my stomach.

What if when I stomped it, it grabbed onto my foot and took a big bite. Then I started to think of family and I started thinking this gigantic bug is probably a grandfather to a lot of young not so big flying bugs....this guy is ugly and big and must be really old to be this size of a bug. I'm a grandfather and I wouldn't want anyone to stomp on me. So I'm watching the Beetle for a while and in his best efforts he is not going to get over on his feet ever again he just keeps spinning around and around......I start feeling sorry, but still careful and very paranoid of the Big Beetle....so I think of a way to scoop him up and get him back into flight....to another country.... or just back to the forest with the rest of the Beetles. I go and get a broom and a dustpan.....now looking at him up close I feel like I should smack him with the broom and get this over with...Nope...I scoop him up, but I am holding him on his back with the broom so he won't jump up and get me!!!! I kind of get a little wheezy while I am bringing him to the edge of the property...to the outside of the gate...very carefully I flip him on his belly and wait for him to get me, but he just stays there...He looks up at me like with the look of are you going to stomp me now? I back up a bit so he can start to feel safe then all of a sudden he starts his engines and takes off.... As I watch him...he gets higher and higher and I think he looked back and waved...I feel like I did a good deed and the beetle family doesn't have to mourn the death of their Grandfather today.......
The next day Jane and I were taking a shower...*to save water*...and when I got out of the shower Jane yells "Earl come back here and look" Yup a big Tarantula or something very similar...big ole harry legs...I ran in my room and got my topsiders on and I did stomp this one...no regrets at all...then the next morning I was leaning down to close up my suitcase and there was a scorpion trying to get in the suitcase and go home with us....KILLED IT! What a great vacation!!!!

BEACH BOYS

Went on a family vacation to Santa Cruz last week....yup my whole family....my 4 kids their wives and my 4 grandchildren and my hip. At last the quiet laid back vacation I've been waiting for all year. Quiet.......laid back.....NOT this week....but fun....Yup! You know I still feel 30 and so when my boys decided to go boogey boarding I was right out there with them....The life guard let us know that we should be careful because there were larger than expected swells coming in for a few days.... He was right...you know about boogey boarding right? You wait out in the ocean (very cold) and all of a sudden you see some swells coming and you start to paddle out to meet them.....But they meet you first....they pick you up and grab you...twist you...turn you.... grind you against the sand...and when you think you can stand up... you are upside down....when you finally get upright the next wave hits and it's fun all over again until you can get to shore.....what a great sport...You know all this shark stuff really gets to me when I'm supposed to be enjoying myself...I'm thinking about Jaws....I don't even want to see the new movie out about the ocean...I was out there the other day and minding my own business and all of a sudden a large seal pops up about 5 feet away.....I know his buddy the shark is just a few feet behind him and looking for his lunch.... so I start paddling to shore as fast as I can and totally by mistake...I catch a wave and ride down the face of it and have what turns out to be an awesome ride....I'm totally focused on the sharks chasing me and ride the waves like I'm the menu, so I make it to the shore as fast as anyone could...had a blast...spent the rest of the day playing on the sand and watching out into the ocean to see if any of my kids were missing.... Looking forward to my vacation from my vacation.....

HO, HO, HO, HO, A PIRATE'S LIFE FOR ME

Does it seem that we have been socked in with fog and cold and wind and rain for just a little too long? Isn't that the start of my last month's story? Yes it was…and nothing has seemed to change….except for just a little more rain. My weeds in my backyard are a real reflection of the amount of rain…I'm glad we don't have any pets we could never find them again after going outside. Well we took another trip…yup another trip to somewhere warm…we headed to Florida and when I looked it up on weather.com it said that for the week we would be gone it would be between the range of 74 and 80 degrees…Just as I have said before….someone is getting my travel plans….we got to the airport and it was warm…. got a convertible to enjoy the sun….after the week was over we realized we should have gotten a car with a sun roof…somehow the weather had changed and even though we did have a couple of good days by far the most were a little cool and rainy. We did some pretty exciting stuff while we were down there….We went to Disney World….and now I know why they call it Disney World….because what else would you call a theme park that has 3 lane freeways running all through it? I spent just as much time making up my own ride….called the "I'm lost here in the park and I can't seem to find anything." I'm not sure what the peak season of Disney East is, but I bet it was the week we went…..I felt like we were playing human bumper cars to get through the Magic Kingdom….the only magic was getting from one end of the park to the other….I loved the part of wanting to go on a ride….you walk up and there is a sign that tells you how long you will wait until you get to the front of the line…and I think that sometimes they were using real slow clocks….at one point we walked up to a ride that said 95 minutes…

I guess they keep it to minutes so as to confuse your children and you...where I live that means I will be standing in line with thousands of people and lots of little people who really don't want to go on the ride anyway, for quite a long time....I believe if they put one hour and 35 minutes they wouldn't have so many people in line...It had been quite some time since I had been to Disneyland in L.A., but I do remember Pirates of the Caribbean and as I recall it was kind of a long ride....like 5 or 6 minutes or so....So when we got to the line for the Pirate's ride in Florida.. 40 minutes didn't seem so long to wait...now I can't say that I was really excited about hanging out with thousands of people being headed to the front of the line through all the maze of metal gateways....it reminded me a whole lot of cattle going to slaughter....when we finally got to the boat to take us on the long journey we jumped in and took off.... Ho Ho Ho Ho it's a pirates life for me....half way through the ride we were stopped because of heavy traffic ahead...kind of like what the pirates probably went through in days gone by......as soon as we started going again...we were done....hey wait a minute...what about the part where we go by the restaurants and all the fire flies are buzzing around....I was pretty let down...although the song HO HO HO HO stuck in my head for at least five full days...we were there in Florida on a business convention with Coldwell Banker and as I was sitting in my classes I was noticing people looking at me funny....and then it would hit me....I was humming out loud my favorite Pirate song....HO HO HO HO a little embarrassing. Maybe I should have bought one of the patches for my eye at the gift center and they would have understood. I guess the fact that I'm a little older than the last time I went to Disneyland it didn't have the same impact...plus we didn't have any kids with us.....it seemed like we were fighting our way into a concert to see some famous band or a million dollar give-away to the first 5 million people who attended the park that day. Oh one last thing.....the food....if you can call it food....Jane was lucky enough to have a Cuban sandwich at one part of the park and I can tell you that if a Cuban eats this sandwich...they are going to think we don't like them and that's why we named it after them...and if Walt could wrap his taste buds around this very poor imitation of a George Foreman grilled bread on bread sandwich...he would probably close down the park and start over.. BYOF....bring your own food...you got it....bring in your own basket or backpack of real food....if you don't eat it all...auction it off to the highest bidder...and pay for your tickets in...which for us it was about $125 a day....for 2.

THE DUKE IS BACK

Hey….how ya been? Good I hope…Next month is going to be a landmark for myself and I can feel the discounts coming. I'm going to be 55…it's really hard for me to even write those numbers down…I still feel about 30 and I know I act like I'm about 16 sometimes. Remember…when about 4 years ago I was going to start counting backwards….well that would make this birthday my 50th. I kinda like the idea of the 55…It's harsh but what the heck…so now I'm starting to plan for the next 5 years and here are a few of the things I would like to accomplish….Do you think this is a mid life crisis at 55 which would mean that I'm going to live to 110? Who knows, but I have this wild idea of hanging out on beaches all over California, Hawaii, Mexico and Costa Rica……SURFING…….yea you got it surfing. When I was in High School I had a long board and would head to Santa Cruz quite often….wasn't any good…and I can only say that now….If you would have asked me 20 years ago I probably would have told you a story about me and Duke surfing the pipeline….the girls sure liked it….I know the dudes knew I was lying, but.. hey It's time to come clean. This year I'm going down to Mexico and take surf lessons from someone who can teach an old dog….new tricks. I rented the video Riding Giants and it really got to me. So now I'm buying surf T-shirts, stocking up on the Sex Wax….(that's the stuff you rub on your board to keep you from slipping off) and getting an extra pair of surf Jams and new Van's for the toes. Maybe I'm taking this thing too far….The last water sport I was going to be a champ at was wind surfing right here in Benicia…I got so excited…started visiting all the wind surfing shops…meeting all the locals who were into it…hanging out on the shores….even bought a nice board with all the gear....I remember hanging 10 at the end of the board in my garage.....no wind...no water....no guts....no go! Sold the gear and was looking for some new adventure....maybe not so cold...not so wet...and not so much energy to go back and forth...back and forth...back and forth...Well this time I really feel like It's the real deal.....I'm bringing the Duke back....the Duke of Earl....Shootin the curl with Earl...Hanging on the beach with Earl's Girls... growing some Earl's Curls...(Mullet) Yeah I can see it now...soaking up the sun...waiting for the Big One....hanging out with young folks around 15 to 18...sitting on our boards talking about life..... wait a minute....what the heck would we talk about? Maybe I could offer up some good old drug counseling to make their day better.... or maybe I could talk about getting a good job and gettin serious about life....Yeah I can hear 'em now...."hey here comes that Old Dude with the Mullet who thinks he's really cool....He'll want to talk to you about the dangers of smoking weed and getting a job..... pretend you speak Spanish and you don't speak English and he'll go away....I heard he flunked his Spanish class. He's always in the way when a good wave comes along....and won't stop talking about the Good Ole Day's!" Well maybe it will be different.....I'm going to give it a try...but this time I'm going to take lessons first and buy the board if I ever catch a wave. Got an e-mail that Maverick's was on last month.. and I couldn't wait..NO not to surf....to watch.... thought I would catch the "Flea" and Clark doing their thing....big big big insane wave surfing. Couldn't sleep after I knew the contest was on.....I woke up at 3 in the morning and headed down to Half Moon Bay....I thought everybody would be there before me and I wanted to get a good spot to watch the competition....I was the first guy there....yup me and the security guards and the news stations gettin' ready for the day....Hung around by myself for a few hours drinking coffee and thinking about the big competition. Stopped at Maverick's surf shop...which was open O-YEAH...got a couple of T's and headed out to the beach....me and the darkness....walked around for a couple hours till folks started showing up....yeah I was excited....maybe a little too excited! I was really hungry...didn't think ahead...had a foot long hot dog at about 8am and had a belly ache all day. The competition was great...thousands of people showed up....a local guy from Santa Cruz won....and it made me think....maybe just maybe someday....I could enter a competition for Senior Surfers....Or maybe I'll just sit on the beach with my board sex wax it up and soak up the sun and thank GOD I made it to 55.

PINEAPPLE EXPRESS

Does it seem that we have been socked in with fog and cold and wind and rain for just a little too long? Well I'm sick of it and decided a few weeks ago that I was not going to take it anymore. I was slowly going into a deep depression and had visions of walking on the beach somewhere with the warm breeze hitting my face and my body turning from bright white to a golden brown. I was watching the TV when I had finally had it. They were talking about a storm coming that only comes once every generation. That was enough for me to make some quick decisions. Then they said it was so bad that there was even a storm coming our way from out at sea called the Pineapple Express. Now I was scared and fed up. So I got on-line and looked on the weather channel and found the hottest spots in the United States..... Palm Beach, Florida was going to be 80 degrees for the next week and Kona Hawaii was going to be a 85 degree hot and beautiful week....So I didn't even call Jane I just booked a flight...We had to get outta here. I knew she wouldn't mind. So I went on-line to book a hotel and found a great one...well it looked great in the pictures. The flight was to LA on a puddle jumper and my mind must have gone blank when they were talking about the Pineapple Express storm.....Had I gone mad? Where would the Pineapple storm be coming from? You got it Hawaii....So we get on the plane to LA and guess what...you got it....the storm was blowing the little plane all over the sky. I knew we were in for some trouble when the pilot said over the loud speaker that the flight attendants would not be getting up from their seats during the flight....because of the turbulent skies. What a dork...I could have been flying away from the storm to Florida not into it...the deciding factor was just 5 degrees! I deserved this...I prayed all the way LA. We made it...Yeah! So now we are waiting for the plane coming to pick us up and take us right smack into the Big Pineapple Storm in the sky. Maybe I should consult others before I make big decisions after all I will be 55 this year and my brain isn't quite up to speed lately. It was rough and we did some dips and shakes, but we made it....Yeah we made it. Now we get the rental car...put the top down and it's 85 outside.....Heaven... yup Heaven...I just love the heat. So we drive to the Huge hotel right on the water with our ocean front room. Which the lady over the phone said was so close you get a mist from the waves...what could be better? Well we got to the hotel and it looked great from a distance...My first indication that things weren't up to par was the valet parking without a valet. Went to the desk to check in and it appeared a bit weathered...It was old and beat up...but huge and right on the water...The lady say's the room I booked was a smoking room and would I mind? Would I mind....I can't begin to tell you how much I mind, but I said I would get some spray and everything would be fine...Went to the room and I have to tell you...this was the worst room I have ever checked into...Smelly, Musty, broken everything, dirty, dirty, dirty, door didn't lock, moldy...Yuck, Yuck. Went back to the desk and checked out. Asked the lady if there was another room I might like better and she smiled and said maybe you should check into the Sheraton...I said OK...gave us directions and we got to the Sheraton and it was a brand new hotel right on the water...way out of town, but clean. The first thing we did was get the bathing suits on and headed to the pool. We only had about 3 hours of sun left, but it was great...The next day we got to the pool early and stayed all day. It was 85 and wonderful...woke up the next morning and it was dark out...Monsoon...I think is what they call it...a change in the weather...Looked like the Pineapple Express turned around when it found out I went to Hawaii...RAIN,RAIN, and WIND, and more WIND and SO STRONG it blew everything that was not attached into the pools...everything went into the pool the chairs, the tables, the plants, the trees and it started getting cold, and it kept raining......all day and night...there was nothing to do except stay in the room...Kinda what I would have been doing at home...the next day which was the day we were leaving it was the same...all day...it finally broke into a sunny afternoon...we got about 3 hours of sun and then had to head to the airport....so we got about 14 total hours of hot sun....but it was just enough to lift our spirits...Next time I have a bright idea...I'll just drive to Walnut Creek...I hear it's been sunny over there for the past couple of weeks! Duhh!

MY FIRST SURF COMPETITION

Well the birthday boy made it home safe and sound...or should I say safe and round! Went down to Huntington Beach for my 55th birthday and had a blast....I spent most of my time in restaurants trying out the food from the Southern culture...One of the reasons I went to Huntington was to live out a dream I had about surfing at the Huntington Pier on my 55th. Driving down to So Cal in our convertible was a lot of fun...we stopped in Carmel to pick-up some of Jane's new art....Did you know you can still buy a home (fixer upper) for only a million dollars in Carmel...Yup a 2 bedroom 1 bath around 900 Sq Ft. bungalow. It was a hot sunny day and we had the top down and were enjoying life...Well if you have been following our trips lately...you know what happens next...yea....black clouds and rain...A few people in Carmel recognized us and asked us to leave town when they saw the clouds coming....So we left...about 2 or 3 miles out of town we pulled over real quick and put up the top.....Rain,Rain,Rain.... Cold rain....heater on...top up and heading to the beaches.. to the land of the sun. You got it....Rained all the way down and when we got to Huntington....Cold, oh so Cold. A miracle happened the next day...we woke up and I believe the weather gods didn't know we were there....It was sunny and a little bit warm..Have you ever bought a hotel on-line? Well I left the reservations to my daughter and Jane....So when I read where we would be staying I only saw.... Beach Street..Now if you are like me you would assume that you would be by the beach....NOT...how about 5 miles from the beach...now if I'm going to the beach for 3 days...I would like to be by the beach......So I went online and got to Priceline.....I put in a bid to stay at a four star hotel for the next couple of nights and for a room at the Hyatt In Newport that costs almost $300 a night I got it for $100.....We left the Beach hotel without even telling them we wouldn't be there for the next couple nights. I called my son who lives in Newport and told him he could stay at the rooms we had rented and he and his girl did. I was in Heaven....Close to the Pacific Coast Highway full service and high dollar hotel and now I'm happy. OK so the first night there I am eating at a local restaurant and I meet this guy who told me he was a great surfer and I tell him my dream of surfing on my birthday...He say's hey Dude...I'll take you out tomorrow...and so I get all excited...I say hey Dude that would be totally cool...he says...Dude we are going to have a blast...I say dude I can hardly wait. He calls me in the morning and say's Dude I can't make it today but, we can hit the waves the next day.. I say hey Dude that would be great and guess what....he doesn't call me...so the next day some friends and I are having dinner and he shows up and tells me Dude I'm sorry...and say's Dude I'll pick you up at 7:30. So I'm all excited and I say Dude that would be great and so I'm sitting out in front of the hotel in the morning and now it's 8:00 and I get a call.....Dude I'm so sorry...someone parked behind me and I can't get my car out...so dude call your son have him pick you up and come to Huntington and we will pack the boards up from my garage and hit the waves. I call my son to come pick me up and he shows up in his work van and we drive off. We get to Huntington and now the surfer Dude won't answer his phone...I have no idea where this idiot lives and it's a good thing cause all I want to do is smash his face and now I'm totally bummed...My son and I go down to the water and watch the surfers and a beach shop opens and I see the board of my dreams for rent...about 5 inches thick and about 11 feet long and bright blue.... I'm in Heaven...I tell my kid what the heck let's go for it and I get on the wet suit and head out to catch the big one. Headed out to where there weren't too many surfers around...as I was paddling out I was just trying not to die...the waves were really huge...really...a few of them came crashing down on me and I ended up back at the beach...as I was laying there my son comes up to help me and I tell him I really don't want to go anymore and I'm exhausted. I tell him that I write the stories and I can make up a good one cause I already went out and paddled around. He says no let's go do it and I agree. So we avoid going towards the pier because there are about a million surfers around it. So looking at the whole scene I decide to paddle out to where there were only a few people surfing. I paddled out to the big ones and every wave almost kills me and I get to where I am going and no one was around except a few dudes. I finally felt safe, but I was totally exhausted and worn out. As I was paddling into a wave trying to avoid getting killed a guy catches the wave and is coming right at me and yells at me and says…what the hell are you doing? You.@##$@!#$$$%…so I yell @##$%%#@$% ,,,and then another surfer comes down the next wave towards me and he starts swearing at me and now I'm pissed and yelling back at him and flipping him off. All I am trying to do is not get crushed by these great big waves. I paddle up over the next huge wave and I see another two guys who are yelling at me and now I am totally pissed off and thinking what a bunch of asses…what do they think…..do they own the waves down here or what……..and then my world, not the waves, came crashing down on me…From the beach which I haven't been able to look back at because of trying to stay alive and go over all the waves…..I hear over a **very loud** loudspeaker…*Sir what are you doing?* I hear it again Sir what are you doing? **You are in the middle of a surfing competition..** could you get out of the area please! I balance myself on the board and I look towards the beach and see a bunch of Budweiser tents and radio station tents and towers and ESPN tents and cameras and T.V. station tents and tons of people standing and staring out to the waves and the surfers I am with and I realize I have blown it bad. The guy comes back on the horn and says…start paddling away from the area…so I start to paddle as hard as I can and I am going no where….then he says.. not that way…that's against the current and you will be in our way all day…turn your board around and do us a favor and paddle towards Long Beach…so I turn around and now I'm paddling really hard to get away and then he comes back on the horn for one last dig..

and says why don't you do us all a big favor and paddle all the way to Long Beach. My son comes up and says hey did those guys yell at you and I tell him what was going on and we laugh. We paddle in and when we are going by all the people we walk fast and keep looking towards the competition so nobody will recognize us. You know it was pretty weird and very embarrassing but, all I can say is…I was in my first surf competition and probably on ESPN at the age of 55. Surfs up Dude!

FAMILY VACATION FUN

Ok, I hear everyone got a real kick out of me out in the surf...You know when I think of the stuff that happens to me I sometimes wonder....does this kind of stuff happen to anybody else? I hope not...well I have news for you....the month of June 2005 has been pretty uneventful. I did however go to Clearlake....did I say Clearlake....I know what you are thinking right now......well things have changed....a little...I rented some brand new cottages on the water in Lower Lake...Now...not a whole lot has changed in Lower Lake...It is nothing like Huntington Beach, but we had to get away and we did for 4 days. The lake was fun.....especially when the wind wasn't blowing...of course the wind was blowing and a major factor in our time off. If it wasn't blowing...it would have been a rain storm or a freak hurricane or twister or something just to make me feel at home. The wind at one point was blowing hard enough to make the waves big enough to surf on, but I left my board at home all I had was my pontoon boat.....the one with the huge 9.9 horse engine. Yes, we had the small engine put on to float around our lake at Hidden Valley (Jeff Dennis calls our lake a pond)...which you can only go 5 to 7 miles an hour on...well you take a pontoon boat out to Clearlake against the wind with that mighty of an engine and you can get up to speeds of at least 3 to 4 miles an hour. So off we went to the other shore headed to the Konocti Harbor which we could see from our beach. Loaded up all the grand kids and their moms and dads and set out for our 3 hour tour...after about an hour it looked as though a few more days and we would be safe at harbor at the Konocti, so everyone voted and we decided to head back to our place...that took another hour...I do have to say...I do have the fastest boat at Hidden

Valley.…..I guess I will keep it there. My kids rented an extreme ski boat for the day for a whopping 500 dollars, but the wind made it almost impossible to wake board.…so they found a real quiet calm cove where the signs said (NO WAKE PLEASE) it was a five mile an hour area.…so being my kids.. they wake boarded there.…they are nothing like me…really.…it really made all the fishermen happy and they seemed to like the kids having fun.…... and they must have thought my kids were professionals because they kept holding up one finger.…I guess signaling them that they thought the kids were number 1. The kids also told me that they heard that the sound of the engine and the constant back and forth of the boat help the people fishing because it makes the fish move closer to the shore. I wasn't in the boat to really enjoy all of this fine behavior.….my kids told me about it when they got back.….they thought it was really funny.….I just smiled and went along with the story.….. knowing that in just a few days they would be going home.….and we would all be getting together next year for our family vacation. Oh those family vacations.…so relaxing.…Oh it's good to be home!!!

WHO WANTS TO BE A MILLIONAIRE?

Ever dreamed of winning a million bucks, or even 20 million bucks, or let's say 60 million. Well about 2 months ago when Jane and I went to Huntington Beach we stayed at the Hyatt in Newport Beach. We had a great time (that's when my surfing career started back up). Well the day we were checking out I left my 2 winning tickets (I still believe they were the ones for 60 mill) on the table when we checked out. Have you ever gone somewhere on a trip or vacation and thought this is the time to buy a lottery ticket….. It seems like for some reason because you are away this is going to be it…The big one! Well I had that feeling about those tickets, so when I remembered that we had left them Jane immediately called and talked to the housekeeping department. They said they would check the room and see if they were there while she was on the phone…..THEY WERE! Yeah….O boy…we were going to be rich…. The guy asked Jane if we wanted them to ship them overnight or just put them in the mail….we were still a few days away from getting home so she said…just mail them…we got home and I waited almost a week…..no letter from the Hotel….I called…. thinking to myself….what if they were the winning tickets….would I if I were the maid or janitor send them to someone I didn't know, or would I cash them in and fly to the Bahamas and live the life I had always dreamed of? Well you make the call!…..So I talked to the guy again and said….did you send the letter with my lottery tickets in it? He said he had and they should have gotten to me by now. YES they should have….Now call me stupid, but when is the last time you sent a letter and it didn't get to where it was going? I have mailed thousands of letters and to this day I believe every one of them got to their destination. I never received my letter and the next week I called again and the guy tells me.....I don't know what to tell you...OK maybe it was the postal service (I doubt it) I looked on-line to see if the big prize was won and....it was, but not in Huntington where I bought the ticket....but maybe just maybe..... it was the 5 out of 6 and it was just for a few million.....I can just imagine.....This guy has probably quit his job and is now making people wait on him.....staying at the hotel in the suites ringing up room service and housekeeping every hour...for the next couple of months....deciding where to go on vacation.

OK...here is an update....we went back to Huntington a few weeks ago to our friend Jessica's wedding...if you remember back she was the one who set my face on fire......first off....have you ever sat in the last seat in an airplane? It doesn't go back, but the one in front of you does....I guess I deserve this for getting to fly first class over the years because of my daughter Jodie. We get up in the sky and the lady in front of me pushes her seat button and..... Boom....her head is practically in my lap.....really....I can count the hairs on her head....she's older and doesn't have much hair. Now you know that our friends have planned this beach wedding by going back 100 years to look at the weather on this date and it was always hot no wind and sunny............It started off OK, but boy did it get cold and windy....I didn't tell anyone at the wedding that everywhere I go I bring bad weather....they wouldn't have invited me.....and I had to get back down there to find the hotel dude.....I had to find out if he was living the life I have always dreamed of. We went to the hotel and checked in...right away I thought they knew I was there, because when I checked in.....out of about 500 rooms... they put us right smack dab next to the air conditioning unit that cools the entire hotel, or maybe the entire coast.....it sounded like a jet was taking off in the next room over...Yup...they knew I was back....I went back up to the front desk and asked to have my room moved and they acted like......what's the big deal....a little noise... OK where is he? Where is the guy with all my money? Well I never found out...but I still think about it....if only I would have picked up those tickets....I wouldn't be writing this story because I would be eating mangoes and pineapples on some warm tropical island. OH well...

THE LAST FAREWELL TOUR

This last month was a whirlwind tour all around the United States. First off it was a long awaited evening with the **Diva of all Divas'**..you guessed it **CHER**..Tickets sold out fast and of course Jane and I only found out she was coming to town long after that. Lory a friend who I work with was really excited and told me I had to go. Lory is the Cher of Coldwell Banker...and she sings **if I could turn back time** at the office quite often and off key but with love and a lot of feeling. Well all the hype about this being her "Farewell Tour" we had to go see her...Kinda like seeing Elvis, or the Who, or Michael Jackson on their "Farewell Tour"...I know they say it is going to be the last time, but we've heard it before. We believe that this really is it for CHER....for the amount of money we had to pay it had better be her farewell tour or I'm going to sue her. What a night...the evening was all that we expected it to be and more. Call me stupid, but I didn't know she had invited every gay person in SF to the concert. There were at least 20 Cher's walking around the Coliseum, and they were HOT, but none of them were female. The one thing that made the concert a little hard to enjoy was a **CHER wannabes** behind me. This guy right behind me and my ears could **clap harder** and **longer** than any other person at any concert in history....and he knew **every word to every song**...Yes...he clapped (**extra loud**) and sang **every word (very loud)** to every song and clapped and screamed (**very loud**) all night long. At first I was so upset that it was ruining my concert and I was thinking about asking him in between songs to knock it off. I would lean way up in my chair so maybe he would get the message, but I think it made him clap harder and closer to my head. At one point I was thinking about turning around and throwing a sucker punch and knocking him out. I finally decided to confront him and turned around and stared at him for a minute in his leather outfit and realized that he was with about 15 other guys all dressed the same and all looked like they just left the gym all buffed and all smiling and I knew right then and there the best thing for me to do was to turn back around and clap and sing as loud as I could for the rest of the concert or get beat to death by 15 bodybuilder die hard Cher fans. After I lost my bad attitude I really enjoyed myself, but that doesn't mean I'm going to go buy leathers.

IT'S A MYSTERY

It's November…and I'm looking forward to Thanksgiving and family and pumpkin pie and mashed potatoes and yams and some turkey! Speaking of Turkey……..I have a great story about one of my new doctors helping me meet the golden years with confidence. Lately you have all been a part of the ongoing Hip and Back troubles…………..Let's throw back in the Shingles….Yup shingles….this is the 9th time I've had them. If you have ever had shingles you will know what I'm talking about when I say they hurt…really hurt and are very unforgiving when it comes to the constant pain……..So I go to see my doctor and this would be the first time with this doctor to share with him my little problem. I go in and the nurse tells me to strip down to my underwear and I tell her that my shingles only stay inside my body not on the outside. She looks at me like I'm crazy….I am. So the doctor comes in and says so how's the hip? So I tell him the whole hip story and he looks happy and then I tell him why I'm at the hospital. He asks me what symptoms I have…. and I tell him about the belt around my side to my back that feels like someone just ripped off all the skin and then begins to electric shock my skin. I tell him that this time the shingles have taken over my entire body…my eyes, ears, legs, and every other part of me. He looks at me like I'm maybe a little crazy…I am….but not so crazy about shingles. If you have had shingles 9 times…you have been to at least 5 different doctors… specialists…MD's…Skin Doctors…everyone was baffled, but put my mind to rest to at least give my condition a name….SHINGLES! That's right….shingles. Up until last week….The doctor looks at me and says….what you have is not shingles…..I ask…then what is it? He looks puzzled at best…and then he says…………..It's a mystery to me! OK....let me see....if it's not shingles....then it's a mystery disease? I'm confused...how about you? I ask if the mystery stuff I have can spread? He say's I don't know....Then I ask how long do you think I am going to have this mystery stuff? He say's.....how long has it lasted in the past? I say about 4 to 6 weeks....then he say's...well why don't you just let it run its course. I'm confused beyond belief at this point. Am I going to die? Is it SARS? Could it be the same contagious virus that is killing all the birds overseas? He seems very calm about my new mystery disease, but I'm not happy at all. At this point he decides to talk about my hip again. He say's you know...if you want to get to the bottom of the problem you have to tell the doctor you want answers. Tell him that you can't go on without knowing what's wrong with your hip and you need to know whether or not you need a replacement. I'm thinking....hey wait a minute.....what about you? Didn't you just tell me that my disease was a mystery? Maybe I should tell you that you need to get me some tests and maybe look into maybe figuring out what I really have if I don't have shingles. Well I don't say anything because.... He's the doctor and for some weird reason.....I just go with what he says. I think we all do that....don't we? We kind of put all of our trust in the doctors, because when you are hurt or sick....you want to get better....no matter what....and they seem to know more than us! If I don't write a column next month you will know that the mystery disease killed me. Hope to see ya!

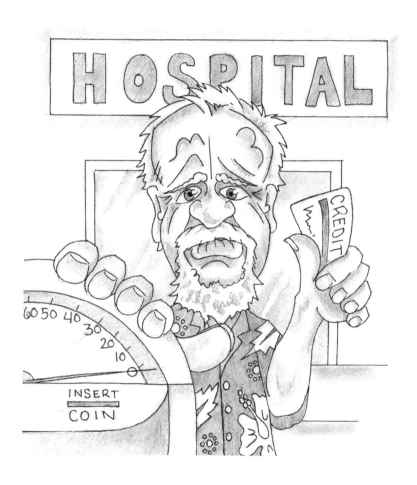

SPARE CHANGE

Hey last week I had to go to Redwood City...to see a specialist for my spine operation......I've heard I was spineless and this proves I'm not...you know you don't get out much when you have to ask someone where is Redwood City? I took off two hours early so I could look around the area when I got there a little early and kind of relax....Not a chance... It took me two hours to get there....there was bumper to bumper traffic everywhere...It reminded me of all the people who have to leave an area because a hurricane is coming...and this is regular traffic.....I really couldn't believe it....my relaxing ride turned into a small panic attack...people aren't as kind as I thought they were on the road. By the time I got to the hospital I was a stressed out wreck...and then it was time to find a parking spot.....I could have made my appointment on time if it wasn't for the parking....I drove around and around and I was getting mad really mad.....nobody was feeling my pain....finally I found a spot not too far away from the hospital....It was a parking meter spot and I had no quarters no dimes no nickels....not even a penny..I didn't want to miss my appointment so I parked and went on to the hospital...I went inside to get some change when I realized I had no money at all. I stood in line in the gift shop trying to buy some candy so I could get some change...they didn't take debit cards...I was beside myself....I asked the lady if there was an ATM machine and she directed me to one down the hall....while I was running around trying not to get a ticket my doctor was waiting upstairs. I get some 20's and went back into the gift shop...now there are a bunch of people in line.... I'm freaking out...I'm gonna miss my appointment....I get in the elevator and go upstairs...when I get to the check-in desk the girl say's "we have been waiting for you"…..I proceed to tell her the story about my trip over to the hospital in the traffic and my parking dilemma. She tells me to try to relax for a few minutes and takes my blood pressure and my temperature and tells me I better go put some quarters in the meter. She tells me she is going to have the doc wait until I get back after I pay the meter. *I guess she could sense the uneasiness in my actions.* I ask if she has any quarters and she says no so I head out. I go downstairs and there is nobody in line, but the lady in the gift shop is on the phone….with someone from her family…I could tell, because she made me wait long enough…. I knew at this point I would have a ticket…I looked at her with the (you better take care of me right now look)…..She Did! I paid for my candy went out to my car and….no ticket…I was relieved…back up to the doctor's office….I explain the whole episode to him….he says he's sorry, but he tells me I will have to come back next month…I tell him….that will probably not happen and is there any way I could avoid it…..NOPE! So I will have to make the trip once again and find parking for a few days when I come back. I guess I will leave the day before and bring a whole pocket full of change. I am setting the date in February for the spine operation…they say there is a good chance I might feel my leg again….MIGHT! Yup….he said it could help, but it might not….Well if I want to be in another surf competition in Huntington Beach next year I figure I better get it fixed.

GARLIC BREATH

They used to be called the Sky Concerts, but now are KaBoom. I never went before because I always seem to think the worst about events like this one, (too many people—rowdy crowds—loud aggressive unkind thugs) but I am here to admit **I WAS WRONG!** What a great night out this turned out to be. First off we started off on the Bart train—which was quiet except for me, and my neighbors. I started a conversation with the people sitting next to me- and we were having fun, and then I noticed we were having too much fun—the lady started to hit me every time she wanted my attention—you know that light tap on the arm to get your full attention, and if you don't respond the attack gets more forceful, and if there is a long sentence or story they hold your arm until they're done. What was so totally ironic about this form of conversation- The couple I went with have this same thing going—whenever one of them is going to speak—I get hit, or held depending on how important the conversation. What's up with that? Why not use my tactic—talk real loud, and cut everyone else off!!! The show was great, the food was great, but 45 minutes in line was not my idea of dining out. (Bring your own food) Jane and I wanted to bless someone in line and buy them a bucket of garlic fries so they wouldn't have to wait—so we walked up to a friendly looking girl about 3/4's back in the line which meant about a half hour...and asked if she was in line for fries—she said yes—so we gave her the bucket, and she says "I was going to buy two" so Jane gives her hers. Well the girl stands there like a deer in headlights—We assure her we haven't done anything totally weird to the fries, but she looks like she doesn't believe us, and we walk away. We continue to spy on the girl and she looks afraid, and won't get out of line. Now I'm thinking of taking back my fries, and giving them to someone else who would appreciate not standing in line for 45 min. Then a guy walked up and she points over at us, and he walks over looking puzzled himself, and says let me pay you for the fries, and we let him know we were just trying to be kind—then he says—well then how would you like something to drink? Hands us a couple of waters, which we took gladly because the fries line only sold hot cider, (go figure). Well the girl finally leaves the line—Garlic Breath and Blessed!

PESO EXCHANGE

Talk about making me sick.......This story is being written right now on a throw-up bag in an airplane headed for Mexico. OK this is what is making me sick.....On our way down to Mexico I thought I would get some pesos at the airport to tip the folks in Mexico upon landing.... like the taxi dude, baggage guys, car rental people, and restaurant folks...kinda to make me feel not so like a Gringo...So I see the sign at the airport in Phoenix and I decide I'm going to get the jump on the Pesos. It seems as though they have decided to make the trip to the money exchange as far as California to Mexico....I start on the journey to the exchange booth.....down the longest runways inside the airport I have ever seen. The people walkers at least made the journey a little quicker especially when you walk on them. I finally got to the money exchange booth. When it was my turn I stepped up to the booth window and the lady in the booth smiled at me and asked..."what can I do for you?" So I tell her I want to buy some Pesos....so I look up at the chart on the wall above her and I see a bunch of numbers.....they really don't mean anything to me until she tries to help me make some sense out of it all. I figure that I will probably need about $50 bucks worth of pesos to start my trip so I tell her "how about $50 dollars worth please?"....and she says..."well it does cost $5.95 to exchange the money and if you want to sell back the Pesos when you come back into the states it will cost you another $5.00." This was definitely a marketing thing they do to make more money. So I figure what the heck....if it's going to cost that much to change my money...why don't I just get $500.00 dollars worth and I won't have to deal with it till I get back. So I tell her...OK give me $500 bucks worth of Pesos. She starts to smile and she hands me a bunch of paper bills and I go away smiling. So now it's back to meet up with the other folks in my party...when I get there they ask me how many Pesos I got for my money and I hand over the slip the nice lady gave me. Now remember she said I could bring back pesos any time for 30 days and get my fair exchange back. Well my wife and friends laugh at me and tell me that I just gave up 60 bucks extra to buy my Pesos and I'm not really happy. So knowing that our plane was soon to take off....I headed back to cash in $450.00 worth of my Pesos. I get on the people mover and I am going about 30 miles an hour on my feet. I get back to the money exchange booth and I wait my turn and when I get to the window I explain how I feel like I was took.... and she asks me what can she help me with....I tell her I want to change my Pesos back in for dollars and she says.....sorry it's too early...I say what? To early...you told me I could change back the money back anytime up to 30 days and get a full refund...Well the nice lady says...."Is there something I can help you with?" I am MAD now and the lady is in a foot thick glass booth...and she can say and do anything she wants...She smiles and ignores me and I want to keep talking to her, but she moved away from the window and will have nothing to do with me....now I have to get back to the plane or miss I'll it...I really wanted to do something about the rip-off, but I had to go. I guess the lesson cost me $60 bucks and a real red face, but I sure won't exchange money at an airport again...

THANK Q

The day we were leaving Mexico and the comfort of our casa we have to get the rent a car...well kinda of a car... they called if full size...a little VW wagon...4 people 8 bags...not full size....So we get packed and we get ready to put the bags in the car and we can't find the key to the car...WE panic and we undo all the luggage.. and no key....we back track for the last 24 hours...I head downtown and go to the restaurant we ate last...Jane goes to the Realty office...Phil goes to a house we had visited yesterday...now we are all in a panic and everyone is running around town....In Phil's travels to the house he passes two people we met the day before...Some guy named Q who just happens to be walking through the town square...Phil stops to tell him of our troubles...about losing the key...and he says...I have the key.... Phil says what? "Yea I think I have your key...he says the guy who sweeps the street found a key yesterday and he gave it to me in case anyone might ask me"....We were totally blown away...this is an absolute miracle...We would have been in a complete mess if their paths wouldn't have crossed at that exact moment....We would have missed our plane and probably had to have someone come pick up the car and charge us about 100 bucks and then got a taxi for about 100 bucks so we were totally blown away. It was getting really crazy just before he came back with the key.....WOW is all I can say.....
THANK GOD—- AND THANK—Q

VENTI WITH A SHOT OF ATTITUDE

We took a trip to Reno a couple days ago and I have to tell you something that happened to us on the way.... I was falling asleep at the wheel and decided to stop and get some coffee to wake me up....I notice a Starbucks sign off the highway and pulled off...We were in Colfax...never been there before...I get to the counter still kind of sleepy and order my Vanilla Cream with a double shot...something I have been ordering for quite some time.....a bunch of people are in line ordering.... there are a bunch of drinks on the counter and the girl keeps yelling out what they are and she keeps calling out a latte...that nobody is picking up.. about 5 minutes go by and I start to think she forgot me, so I go up to the counter and ask her if she forgot my Vanilla Cream and she say's...that's it right there **(with a whole lot of (bad) attitude)**...I say no....that's a latte...she says..."they're the same thing" and looks at me like **I'm some kind of a dummy**....Well all of a sudden I'm not so sleepy anymore...and my drink is no longer hot and **I'm wide awake and mad**.. the caffeine hasn't even hit my system. Now all of a sudden Jane is going through the same thing...and the girl...it appears is picking on us and her attitude has gotten a whole lot worse..Jane and I are looking at each other like...**Let's hurt her**..

All we want to do now...is strangle the girl....so we leave... wide awake...

I guess stopping at Starbucks really does work when you are a little tired. **Need a quick wake up on the way to Reno?** Stop in Colfax. C-YA

OUT TO SEA

I was sitting at my desk a few weeks ago and it was raining and raining and raining and it was cold….did I mention cold? I was really kind of depressed and cold! I was doing a lot of thinking about the major surgery that was about to be performed on my back to my spine. Tell me if this has ever happened to you…in a conversation you tell someone you are going to have surgery and without concern for you they will think long and hard and sometimes I think they have heard a story from somewhere, but don't really know what they are talking about, but they start talking about someone who had a similar surgery and either didn't make it or was totally disfigured or who limps or can't see or talks with a slur or something horrible……Lately I have heard nothing but horror stories…yup..my fellow man building the confidence I need to go get my surgery. Well I start to believe some of these stories and I feel like, if I am not going to make it out OK, I better get in one more vacation, so I head down to Mexico. I had something go wrong with my foot about two weeks before I left, but my doctor was too busy to get me an appointment, so I left for Mexico hurting and limping. One beautiful hot sunny day I was out body surfing and I noticed the waves getting really huge and so I started to swim out further to avoid getting smashed and killed. When I really took notice of what I was doing I realized, I was way too far out away from shore, so I started swimming towards the beach. The waves were smashing on top of me and making it hard to catch my breath. I found myself doing everything I could just to keep my shorts on and stay alive. I was doing cartwheels and front flips and back flips and eating my share of sand. When I finally got to where I could stand up and catch a breath I felt like maybe I wasn't going to die. The water was up to my mouth and I was exhausted. I was staring at the beach praying I would get there soon. All the water I was standing in was being sucked out to sea and all of a sudden I looked behind me and a wave was about to break, right on me...so I knelt down and pushed off and darted straight up like a bullet.....**the wave grabbed me and drove me into the sand like a really sharp#2 pencil..** When my feet hit the sand I thought my foot and leg had shattered and I would never walk again. It took everything I had to get to shore I was being battered and driven into the sand. When finally got to the shore I just laid there totally exhausted thinking I still might not make it. After I caught my breath and was able to think about what just happened It took me about a half an hour on my knees to go about 50 yards in unbelievable pain. I finally crawled up to some tables where some people were sitting and I asked for some help. I told them what had just happened and asked if someone could drive me home. For 2 days I had to be carried around. Left Mexico and got back home and went for my Pre-Op for the spine operation and the doc started to test me and looked startled and said what have you been doing? You have about 50 % more movement in your foot and leg. He asked if it was still numb and I told him it wasn't numb anymore. I told him about my body surfing accident and we both came to the conclusion that something happened out there in the ocean...like the surf Gods knew I needed fixing and they fixed me...yup they really fixed me...He told me that even if I had done an operation on your spine I am not sure you would be in this good of shape. He told me to come back in six months and see if I still was feeling good. The next day I went to a foot doctor and it looks as though I had ripped some tendons a few weeks prior to the surfing accident and the final slam into the sand finished it off. I got a cast up to my knee for the next six weeks and I hate it. The first day I got it on I pulled out my back.....the next day I was over a friend's house and I was pulling my cast around to get seated and I fell off a chair on to the floor....Have you ever fallen and it seems to have changed all the bone structure inside your body.....kinda like the bones are all in a new place and the muscles are finding it hard to help you move....well that's what happened and I could hardly move for 2 days....That's not the end of the cast story....about 3 days later I was at work and I was cleaning up a bunch of cardboard around the Art Gallery and putting it in a dumpster....the dumpster was getting full so I jumped in.....I know what you are thinking....what an idiot.... doesn't he have a cast on? Yup....stupid...So as I was jumping up and down like a mad man and crushing the cardboard.... the extra weight from the cast made the cardboard easier to crush. I slipped when I landed on one of my jumps and when I did.... I bent back the fingers so far on my left hand so that they touched my wrist. The pain was incredibly intense. I didn't want to go to the doctor, because I would have felt kinda dumb when they asked how I did it. The next day my fingers were as fat as ballpark hotdogs and my back felt like someone hit me with a truck and my foot in the cast was really hurting...I think I need a vacation...somewhere hot and at a really nice beach where I could go body surfing and just enjoy the sun and the time off....what do you think?

CASTING CALL

Now for the ongoing saga I think of as the casting call. It was time to get my cast off after a month and I was so looking forward to it. I don't know if I mentioned the pain and agony I have gone through in the last month....but let me let you have a glimpse....The cast seems to weigh about 30 pounds and sometimes even more. Well swinging this thing around threw out my back and made it almost impossible to walk. To add to the agony, my cortisone shot to relieve the pain in my hip was wearing off, so it also started to kill me....so trying to adjust my walking with my back and my hip out I started to notice my other hip start wanting some attention....Yup both hips and my back started working against me. I know I have been hard on my body, but come on. When you read this I will just be turning 56...some of you will say....that's not old...some of you will say WOW he really is old. Whatever....I'm just a boy who wants to surf....I know you have heard that line...kinda....I'm just a girl who wants to paint..(my wife) that pretty much sums up our lives at this point. On to the casting room...I walked in and this doc walks up looks pretty sleepy and says....I'm tired...and I'm thinking Oh...you're tired...try being me for a day...then he say's I've done quite a few of these today. So I don't know if I should feel good or bad about what is going to take place. He cuts off the cast and sends me to my doctor down the hall.....My doctor examines my foot and asks... how does it feel? I lie and say great! Then I ask him if I could get a cortisone shot just for preventative measures...he says yeah and I'm happy as can be. I leave the hospital...in pain, but I'm not telling anyone.....I'm cast free. The next day comes and I'm feeling a lot of pain and a little stupid...maybe a lot stupid. So I call the hospital to get another cast on and they can't help me until Monday. I go in on Monday and go through the whole cast thing and get a new cast on...I think I was moving my foot when I was getting the cast on because...it sure didn't feel right. I didn't say anything, but another doctor saw me walking out and said it looked like I might snap my knee out, so I went back in and they put a wedge in my cast shoe. That fixed it...but that night it felt horrible in bed so the next morning I drove back to the hospital. Yup walked in asked if I could get a new cast...They were OK with it...A new doctor did the honors...he really took his time made it special with an arch to die for...yes to die for...as I am sitting here I am trying to decide whether I should get another cast, because I feel like I have an arch blister the size of the wave that started this whole thing.

CASTING CALL—TAKE TWO

OK let's wrap up the medical news for starters....at the end of the last story I was complaining about the cast and how it was hurting me.....well here is what's happened since.......I really wanted to go and have the cast taken off to relieve me from the UNBELIEVABLE pain....but I couldn't face the idea of going back to see the casting crew. If I would have gone back it would have been my 4th cast and not only would they think I was a big pain in the butt, but every time I went back I requested someone new to put on a new cast and they were out of cast members, so instead of having them fix it I lived with it for 4 more weeks. The thing that was hurting me was not a stone or a spur in the cast.....it was that the cast was to tight and it was squeezing my foot and toes. I did end up with a real nice blister and that was what was hurting. I'm pretty tough when it comes to pain.... as a matter of fact I am much tougher than pain....my wife seems to think it's not that I'm tough....she say's she thinks I'm stupid....really stupid....she kept on telling me to go and have the cast redone, but I told her that I would get through it.....Well.... "I told you so" didn't come out of her mouth, but it should have! I should have gone back.....and the next time I will listen to her....you probably are asking yourself.... what does he mean next time. I don't know if I told you in the other stories....I have had a cast on that foot and leg....at least 5 times in my life. So the likelihood of getting another cast is pretty good. So now I go to the hospital and the casting crew are all smiles when I come in.. The doc comes over to me and has me lift my leg and he looks up at me and says in total disgust....who put this on? The tone of voice I have heard before.....It was kinda like "what DORK who calls himself a doctor put this cast on"? I said the new guy…and the doctors all just laughed…. When the cast got cut off I realized I now had a new set of problems….I couldn't feel my foot or my toes…..It seems as though the NEW guy put the cast on too tight….I think the nerves were damaged…..At this point I think I'm damaged….I'm not sure I should go back to any doctor anymore……So I think to myself….why not get my leg cut off…and get a wooden peg leg…..I could get a job at the Pizza Pirate as the greeter…..AAAAARRRR Ho Ho Ho Ho it's a pirates life for me…. OK…enough of that….I've decided to keep the leg, but I know I need to get a second opinion….What happens if I see the doctor who worked on me before…..if I am limping and he asks "how's the leg….what am I suppose to say? Everything is great "….and what if he walks by when I'm in the new doctors office…..what if they make a plan to keep hurting me and never let me get my leg back to the way it was….OK maybe I am a little paranoid….but how would you feel at your job if someone came in and you gave them an answer to their question and then they asked to talk to someone else besides you to see if they might like the answer better….wouldn't it make you feel kinda weird? All I want is to feel better….I bet if I was a big sports star…I wouldn't be going through this….I would have been fixed and I would probably be winning surf competitions down in Huntington Beach….Well my foot is still asleep and my toes are too and now my heel feels like I just had the accident again……I don't know if you have seen me walking around town lately, but it's not a pretty sight……I can hardly get around without screaming in pain……I guess I'll just bite the bullet and go see the 2nd opinion doctor this week……I sure hope the 1st opinion doc understands…. I really like him and I don't want to hurt his feelings….I really have a good head about this whole thing….I believe I will be much better very soon. I want to go back out to the ocean and body surf and do some Big Wave Dave stuff……maybe God just wants me to sit on the beach and watch the surfers enjoy themselves. Only time will tell, but until then I will do everything in my power to get back up on the big board and hang 10. I'll let you know what happens next month….to cast or not to cast is the question………… Cowabunga………..Dude and Dudettes!

MY POD

OK here goes another story that you can get together with some friends and laugh about. I wanted to sell our house here in Benicia and as a Real Estate Agent I knew what a breeze it would be to sell and move. I just bought the house 2 years ago and put everything I had into it. Yup....money...more money...and yup...more money....did I mention money? Everything had to be just right...the right colors...the right carpet...the right fireplace...the right mantle...the right kitchen...the right granite.... The right fences without knot holes. the right fridge...the right cook's kitchen stove....the right lighting....the right faucets...the right showers....the right jetted tub....the right closet arrangement....the right moulding....the right tile floors....the right shower doors that slide with ease...the right roof...the right colors for the backyard cement....the right decking...the right landscaping...yup you guessed it......the best of everything......Why? You ask why? Well because we were going to live in this house till the end of time.... If you would have told me that the end of time was going to be 2 years I would have laughed. Well it's time to laugh with me...... and yes at me....I was *totally* convinced that we would live in this home forever. On one of our vacations we ventured off to Mexico... yup....Mexico.....dirt streets...ladies selling chickens on the street corners...nobody speaking the only language I know...Here we are at another cross road in our life....what was I thinking....I don't think I was doing any thinking....I think I fell in love with the idea that if I moved here I might get to relax.....Ahhhhh come on...... Relax? I don't know how to relax...but something happened.....I really can't pinpoint it, but something happened....So one day about four months ago I went to my wife Jane and said....Hey honey how about selling our beautiful home that we just finished last week and moving to Mexico? She really didn't have to answer me because I knew the look and I knew the answer....absolutely not....no...no...no...no. So I left that thought in the dusty dirty roads of Mexico... well a few months later I got brave enough or dumb enough to ask once again.....Yea....I'm the little boy who gets his fingers caught in the dresser.....and does it again and again and never learns. Well this time to my amazement she said yes....yup......she said yes..... I have no idea what came over her mind that day, so we started planning and since then we have been here in spirit and down there in our minds.....So we put the home on the market and knowing the market at this time....... it takes a little longer to sell. One day my wife was having a garage sale and a nice young lady asks if she can look at the home and we said sure, so she walked in and she went through the house.....she was in for just a few minutes, but I guess she loved it because.....her and her husband bought it. I think this is the week the bottom dropped out of the real estate market. Ok now the fun begins......Moving......now when I sell a house for a client...I tell them.....Oh the move will be a breeze....just put the stuff in a box and move it into your new home....It's as easy as that....except for all the stuff in-between. OH my God! Where did all this stuff come from? Whose is it anyway? We had to have someone drop off a POD.....what a racquet......everything we didn't use over the last fifteen years goes out in the POD and they whisk it away to some unknown location and we don't really care if they ever come back. We moved in town....less than a mile from our home to our new home. I think I made about 9,000 trips back and forth..... I should have just had a fire sale....yup.....burned all of it without ever looking back. I haven't missed anything in the POD, but I hear it's coming to my new place next week...Maybe, just maybe, they will lose it. Ok the move was unbearable......I swear I don't want to ever move again.....or at least for two more years.......OK it's the last day of moving and I go back and there are only a few plants and some buckets and a few pieces of useless stuff. I park my Tahoe on the steep hill and start to fill it up with stuff from the end of the move.........I lift a 5 gallon bucket it's full...I test the lid...seems to be pretty secure, so I lift it up and put it in the back of the Tahoe.....Nope.......it falls over and the lid comes flying off.....It's the bright red stain for our fences....it is pouring and is spreading all over the back of the car thick stain about 2 inches deep and now is moving under the seats and finally reaches the front seats....5 gallons of smelly stain now my carpets are soaked, so I freak out.... I get the hose and spray the car at full blast for about an hour...the stain is pretty much gone....but the smell will be with me until I move again.

DIRTY ROADS AND DUSTY CHICKEN

OK it's February 2006 and it's cold and dark and rainy and….. oh I'll stop there……you know what it is…I had to get out of here so my bones wouldn't break!!!! I called a friend in Benicia today and they told me it had gotten down into the 20's……OUCH!!!!I'll just let you know that I'm writing this letter and it's 8pm and it's still 75 out and it looks like tomorrow will probably be about 85. Yea you guessed it….back in Mexico…. there is something about this hot weather and the beaches and the surf and these people that makes me want to yell out……I love this place…….I'll get back to that story in a minute, but first…. let's start this story with the news from the end of last year…..As you all know the housing market wasn't all it was just a couple of years ago,…and we had a little time to relax and reflect on what we wanted in our lives and it came down to health…yup health…. without it….you got nothing. So Jane and I are trying to change our whole program….and I must say it sure sounds great, but getting to it is a little harder than talking about it. I just have to take a look in the mirror and know that things have gone a little hay wire……My wife looks great, but the other day while laying on the beach here in Mexico a group of people tried to roll me back into the ocean….I think it was the Save the Whale folks….We bought Yoga mats and Jane has been doing her yoga each morning while I watch….It takes me a little longer to get started..We go to the store and buy nothing but great food….then we go out to eat, a lot…..and the vegetables usually go into the compost pile. I really want this to happen, but I think it's going to be in baby steps. I have been on a diet ever since I have been writing these stories…which has been about 13 years. I have gotten to the weight I want about 10 times, but then I celebrate with a burger and pizza and candy and cake. I bet the day I die they will come up with a pill that lets you control your weight within a pound or two. Came down here on vacation and noticed that they are building a new building right next to my home....yup right next.... they build with your wall....so every morning which means...... every morning.... they show up with their hammers and a generator that has no muffler and they start to pound and mix cement at 7AM sharp...I'm not sure they need to pound on my wall first thing, but I think.... they think it's kinda funny. Being down here is so different than home....one would wonder why someone who would rather sleep at the Hilton than pitch a tent and be with nature would be here. The roads are dirty and dusty....your car turns from whatever color it is.... to dirt brown in a matter of a day or two. There is no real grocery store....no post office...no police...no gas station...no ice cream store....and when you do go to the stores that are here.....if you're lucky someone speaks English...if you are really lucky. I have been working on my Spanish each day....and I hope that soon I will be able to communicate..Just looking at each other and smiling usually just gets both parties frustrated. Went into town the other day and bought a phone for the house......35 miles each way....got back all excited and got home opened the box and guess what? NO PHONE!! Now I get to go back and without speaking Spanish...try to tell them that there was no phone in the box....How do you think it is going to go? We will probably make a whole lot of hand gestures.....pretend to hold the phone up to my ear.....open the box in front of them and look real surprised and with my eyes wide open and a dumb look on my face pull out the paper in the box and..... however you can make a look like something is missing.....throw my hands up and wait for a response.......I now understand what it feels like to be in a foreign place and not be able to communicate..... although....no matter where I go....someone special will always come to my side and try to help...there is a peace down here that is like no other place I have ever been and for once in my life I feel like I belong...and at the same time I am also a misfit....but then I always have been so I should be used to it.

LIT UP LIKE A CHRISTMAS TREE

I just got back from Mexico on a mini vacation....and this is the first time I have gone down there in the summer....Oh my, is it hot! It's a different kind of hot...than like let's say Palm Springs...It's hot and **Humid**...How **Humid** you ask? About once an hour you put on a new shirt and let the other one dry out. Your hair is constantly wet and takes on a whole new look like you just jumped out of the shower. Well I also got to experience a rain and lightning and thunder storm....as you might not know...our casa is located in the Rain Forest...by the beach...I looked down the coast and noticed a real dark cloud formation heading our way.... FAST...the sky turned black real fast...I also noticed a change in temperature....real fast...then it started to rain....not your regular rain....lots and lots of rain....you could say buckets of rain....enough rain that in no time at all the streets looked like little rushing rivers....and then in the distance you could hear the thunder.... NOW.. I have been in thunder storms before...and they were really fun. You know how you see the lightning and then you count one one thousand, two one thousand...that makes it fun and you also realize how safe you are because each one one thousand is suppose to be one mile away for the Zillion volts of electricity pounding down into the earth. Well the louder the thunder got the closer the lightening got....at one point the lightning would hit and you couldn't count even to one. The whole village would light up like a Pro football field at night......and then the thunder...it was so loud that it hurt your ears....and it just kept on coming....at one point I saw the lightning bolts so close I thought it was going to hit me......and then the thunder right behind it......at one point they were coming together...the thunder was so loud that I was looking at our rentals from the balcony of the main house and I thought the building was going to explode into pieces all over me. I swear to you....I was scared to death....this storm didn't just go by in a few minutes like most storms....it stayed with us for about 6 to 7 hours. Scary...scary...scary....It knocked out our electricity for a full day...what was really crazy was the town was still doing business as usual...people were walking in the streets and it seemed like nothing to them...It's weird to me when it's 90 degrees out and it's raining like cats and dogs...lightning is hitting and nobody notices but me!!! See you in the pool with my umbrella!

IT'S A MIRACLE

OK, it's October 2007 and the sun is still up and the weather is perfect. That is why we live here in paradise. This month is going to be kind of a mix match of stories, because I'm actually brain dead. As many of you recall about five months ago I had a body surfing accident in Mexico. Well the result was eight weeks in a cast and after I got the last cast off, my foot wasn't any better and as a matter of fact it was worse. Yup the cast was put on a little tight and to this day I can run my finger across my foot and not feel it. Oh that modern medicine.......what would we do without it? Well I can't remember if I told you that at the end of the whole cast event I went back to the foot doctor he decided to get together with a surgeon and talk about doing a little surgery. At the time my foot hurt so bad I was ready for anything. Well as my schedule would have it I missed the date to talk with the surgeon and I was just about ready to reschedule, but a miracle happened. The pain went away about two weeks later. I call it a miracle....you call it what you want......not having to walk on crutches for four to six weeks makes it a miracle in my book. Now I know we are talking about my feet, but remember my back and my hip are still not worth a hill of beans and hurt always. So when my foot got better it was so great to walk without the pain of sharp knives stabbing into the bottom of my heel with each step. For about three weeks all I had was the hip feeling like it was going to break off and my back went out only about two or three times in the three weeks. When I went to the doctor for my back during that time.... He was kind of blunt and said "you're fat" and "your body can't carry the weight..... so lose it!" That's easy for him to say he's a little skinny guy that probably has no concept of what a cheeseburger and a pizza feel like when you're hurting. Ok it's three weeks later and guess what.…. the weirdest thing happened, the "planter facc cee ites" foot stuff worked its way through my body to my other foot.…I guess it took a vacation and got lost in my body and ended up in the other leg. It is killing me.…now…if you have never had this foot thing.…you will never know what I'm talking about……if you have let's say it together.……… Oooooooooooooooooooouch. I took the doc's advice and went on.…yup another diet.…. I'm back at Weight Watchers and trying once again. I bet the day I die they will come up with a pill to make you the right weight.…now I don't mind eating fruits and vegetables and drinking six to eight bottles of water a day and spending half my day in the bathroom, but I've been down this road before. As a matter of fact I believe I have lost at least four to five hundred pounds over the last fifteen years. No I wasn't 700 pounds…I lose about forty pounds every other year and gain back forty-one pounds the following year. I would say that this is it, but if you or the doctor see me in a month or two at Randy's eating chips and salsa and a big ole burrito you will probably understand that I love to eat. And maybe I love to diet. I really never gave that any thought…maybe just maybe I feel the need to punish myself for all the good eating.…Ahhhhh I'll let you know next month if I'm on the right track. I should go and get a cast on my leg for the foot pain, but I am heading down to Mexico in a couple days and……… you guessed it…body surfing and bogey boarding and swimming in the ocean are my favorite things to do. So I'll go body surfing with hopes of not getting into another accident. You are probably saying "what a dork".….and you are probably right, but if I give up what I love to do you might as well put my whole body in a cast and throw me out to sea. Having a little mid life crisis I bought a Harley the other day. My friend Todd calls it a "skirtster" because it's the 1200 Sportster not the big Hog. I kind of feel like just buzzing around town and saving a little on gas and I know I could never live it down on a Vespa.…so I took the only road I could. If you see me.…. don't wave please…..I can't see that well anymore and if I take my hand off the handle bars to wave….. well, let's just say I don't want to have to start writing about my accidents.

JOEL TURNS ONE

I want to talk to all of you about a party I went to a few weeks ago that kind of made my head spin. My grandson Joel turned one last month and I heard the talk of getting together a few of his little friends for the party. As the talk went on I started to realize that this was going to be the "only time he was going to turn 1" so it needed to be a great party. I'm thinking....do you think he is going to remember this? What kind of games does a 1 year old have at his party? What will the menu consist of....will it be a sleep-over? Should we make it a surprise party and really keep it a surprise? Maybe we could make it a theme party....where everybody could dress up like adults....**that's it**.....Make it a surprise party where everyone shows up as adults.... OK now that makes it a lot easier.... So my daughter tells me that there will be about 60 people at the party so we better get busy with the arrangements. You know I've had 56 birthdays and I only remember one that more than 6 to 10 people came to. So we got ready for the party and it turned out to be a big surprise for Joel....you should have seen the look on his face when all 60 adults screamed **SURPRISE** and Happy Birthday.... He was so happy he cried for a bit.....oh those tears of **JOY**. Call me old fashioned, but this seems as though it might have gotten out of hand somewhere down the line. I did mention to a few that I thought it was a bit of over the top, but I just got those looks of "what do you know old dude"...things have changed since you were one. It really turned out to be a great party and If I ever have another child....his or her first birthday will be a party they will remember for the rest of their lives.

HOW I MET PONCHO VILLA

Wow, what a quick year 2006 was....I'm writing this on December 17th. on a cold but clear evening. Not a creature is stirring not even a mouse .Why? You ask why? IT'S TOO COLD that's all I have to say. Hey sorry.... really sorry about not getting in a story in time last month. I could lie and say I was on vacation, but it wouldn't be a lie....I was on vacation and by the time I realized it was time to send in a story.....it was too late. My phone doesn't work in Mexico...so on my way back I have a layover in Arizona and I retrieve all my messages and it usually starts with "Hey where are ya?" kinda in a nice tone and as the days have gone by towards the end of the week the messages get a little heated like.... "Hey what the heck are you doing? How come you're not calling me back? How many times do I have to call? Are you alive or have you fallen off the Earth?" And some even get a little irate and put in a swear word or two. A lot of these people are the very folks I tell that I will be leaving for a week. This last trip to Mexico was very entertaining....we got our house done that we have been working on for the last 5 months or so. We got the landscape done and furnished it all with the help of good ole Mexican...Sam's club and Wal Mart...yup even in Mexico.. The only difference is that no one speaks English and all the products are written in Spanish...I took a Spanish class and have the books and a bunch of CD's, but it is not coming as fast as I would like. I am making a real effort this year to learn as much as I can because it is very hard to communicate when you really need to. So I have been going down for the last two and a half years and have really gotten into the real estate business down there. It is very different and I love it just as much as I do up here. To find the really prime pieces you have to go on scouting missions…..I started talking to a lot of the locals to give me tips on what to do. So I asked a friend of mine who is helping me with the business to take me out to find some waterfront properties up the coast. One morning my friend Aaron picked me up to go out scouting….We were headed up the coast about 35 miles in a rundown surf van that had no air conditioning and none of the windows rolled down and it was a bit rickety…. not to mention dirty…beyond dirty….nothing but dirt roads and lots of them. So we headed up the coast and we passed quite a few towns…big ones and small villages…..fortunately for me Aaron speaks fluent Spanish which makes things real nice. He starts to tell me stories about Gringos going into villages and never coming out. He starts telling me stories I really don't want to hear. Actually he has me scared to death and I'm feeling like maybe I don't want to go, but we are half way there. He tells me we are looking for this certain man who is a land scout and has some prime pieces, but we don't know where he lives, but we do have his name. Well the village where we heard all the stories about is the village where this scout lives, so we head into the village and start asking for this one guy….. At first nobody wants to talk to us and nobody seems to know where this guy is, but one person sends us to the corner of the village and we get out of the car and yell out his name….the reason we yell is because we don't know who or what is in the house. There is no front door or windows or even a doorbell on this house. A very scary man comes to the door and it looks like he has just been beaten by a gang of people…His eyes are bleeding and all red and swollen and his arm is in a sling and he has cuts all over his body and he is really dirty and he looks really bad. So I think to myself…. Oh my God let's get out of here before it happens to me. He acknowledges us and waves for us to come up to the door. He turns out to be a really nice guy and proceeds to tell us what had happened to him and he tells us that he fell down hauling wood. He ends up telling us he will be helping us find the scout…We head back out of the village to the highway where we are pulled over waiting for the scout. Police go by and stare at us, but probably go on by because we look like surf bums. We have a description of the car the scout is suppose to be coming back to town in so we wait. We see the car coming and my friend gets out and waves him down. He parks behind us and walks up to the van...he pushes open the sliding door of the van and jumps in smiling at me....OH my god this guy has just a few teeth and only one eye...the other one is all white and glazed over and now I'm thinking oh my God....Someone has probably stabbed this guy in the eye and I'm gonna die without anyone knowing I'm out here in this village. We drive him back to the house where we were and he takes us in his house and is one of the nicest guys you ever want to meet. Although I can't understand one word he says...my friend tells me that we are getting along just great. I am having a heat stroke and I am starting to pass out. I go out to the van which is just as hot and pass out on the floor. I wake up a little while later delirious and soaking wet and drooling all over myself. I went back in and excused myself and they all smiled, because they didn't understand a word I said. We are done doing business and get back in the van and we end up going home with about 8 new pieces of ocean front property and a bunch of new friends. After I thought about it for awhile I think my friend was just trying to scare me so I would behave...I did!

PONCHO VILLA GOES G.Q.

I headed back to Mexico the following month and this was the first time I have gone on a vacation in the last 10 years that was longer than 10 days. A little update from the last time I told you about the very scary dude in the little village. I went out to the village with my buddy Aaron again and we were supposed to meet up with the same guy who was the scout for properties. You remember the guy with no teeth and the one eye that was glazed over....very scary...we waited at the entrance of the village again and he pulled up in the same van that he had last time, but this time things had changed. I saw him getting out of the van and the first thing I saw was a brand new pair of very expensive ostrich cowboy boots and some designer slacks. When he jumped out it seemed to switch to a slow motion commercial...I hardly recognized him...He smiled and had a full rack of bright white teeth a real nice shirt and some designer sun glasses and a patch over his eye.....things are looking up for the scout. I know in the village he lived in there was this bad thing about selling property to Gringos so he had to keep quiet about what was going on. He probably told the villagers he had won the lottery, or sold 500 donkeys. He was such a nice guy I was really happy to see the change...Maybe after he sells a few more ocean front properties he will meet us in his helicopter or Hummer. Life is good in Mexico and getting better.

BORN UNDER A BAD SIGN

Almost every time I get the shingles I leave and go to Mexico to get away from the stress and pain. I left the United States with my shingles and my suitcase and I wasn't feeling so good. The first day down there I came out of my new casa and I had forgotten that they put in new curbs. Me and my shingles slipped off the curb and fell to the ground and sprained my ankle real bad. It threw all my muscles totally out of whack and my body was hurting. I was walking downtown later that day and I was having a hard time getting around with my ankle and I was trying to get up a curb and tripped and slipped and fell into a flowerbed and ripped and scraped my leg and I watched it bleed. I knew at that point that I should probably be careful because things were not looking so good for me. I had a sprained ankle and a gash on my leg and my shingles. The next day I noticed that my limping had thrown out my back and my hip was starting to hurt. Just before I left the states I had gotten a cortisone shot to stop the pain and it only lasted about 6 days into my trip. So now my back is out, my shingles are driving me crazy, my hip is killing me I am limping on my sprained ankle and I have a gash in my leg. I thought to myself…nothing else could possibly go wrong…. The next day Jane and I went to a nursery in a little village up the coast and we were there to pick out new palm trees for our house. As I was walking through the nursery the palms were thick and it was really humid and about a hundred degrees and I was hot and soaking wet. We got the palms picked out and we got back in the car and I started to itch and I looked down at my arm and I had about 100 bites on my inner arm and it was bright red and then I lifted my shirt and I had about 200 more bites and it was all bright red also all over my side. I felt horrible and thoughts of suicide entered my mind, but I hung in there. I went to the doctor in our village and he prescribed some lotions. One of the lotions he had me buy had a no human's circle on it and I read it and it was for ticks for dogs. I used it anyway. All the lotions mixed together made me feel a little better. Three days later I was hiking in the jungle and I was bit about 500 more times by what someone called noceems.... No see ems...they are little bugs so small you can't see em. I was out of my mind in pain at this point. It was a real weird feeling...it felt like water was dripping out of the wounds at all times. The next day I was back in the jungle and looking for ocean view properties when I looked down and my leg had this big black large spot on it and I had about 500 tics on my leg...lucky thing Cochin my friend I was with had some yard guard spray and he fogged me up and down and they all died. Now I know what you are thinking right now...what the hell is wrong with Earl....why does he keep putting himself in those kind of places? I had been to the doctor three times in the first three weeks and felt kind of stupid, but I was on a mission. The week before I left I was out swimming in the pool and I put my arm over the edge of the pool and I got a bite that felt like a sharp knife just stabbed me. That night I went to bed and woke up not being able to breath...my uvula had gotten the size of a cell phone and was stuck in my throat and choking me to death. I couldn't believe that all of this was happening to me...I went to the pharmacist in town and he told me that the swelling of the uvula is what happens when you get stung by a scorpion and I was not surprised at all..... I just believed that because I didn't die everything was gonna be ok......wanna go to Mexico with me?

PAIN IN THE BUTT

A couple weeks ago I was feeling pretty good and decided to paint the ceiling of the art gallery.....stretching and moving back and forth and stretching and bending and bending...and rip........my back went out.....not to lunch...it quit it's job....so what did I do? I went home and laid in bed all day and rested and then got up in the morning and what would any full blooded male ding-dong do....I went back to the gallery and started painting again the very next day.....trying to hide the fact that I was severely injured. I really wanted to finish the project I started.... and not wimp out.......after the 2nd day of painting I felt like I was going to die. I couldn't walk, talk or think.......It was the worst pain I had felt in years....the bad thing was my hip was still recovering from an operation and hurt just as bad. Now I have a bad back and a bad hip...hardly able to walk....I still have to go to work...I don't know how to spell sciatic nerve, but who cares....if you have hurt your sciatic you know what I'm talking about...I don't think anything hurts worse......except kidney stones...but that's another story. You can't sit...you can't lie down....you can't sleep....you can't think...you don't know what to do....just hurt.....that's all you can do...I went to the chiropractor three times....helped for a bit but it came back with a vengeance.....went to the doctor....he gave me pain killers.....even went to the acupuncture dude....that seemed to help the most...but it's been two weeks and....I went to the hospital today...they are going to give me an MRI, get some X-Rays, and some cortisone. It's been quite painful, but I know it will someday be better...at least I hope so....It hurts getting older....I guess you could say it's A REAL PAIN IN THE BUTT!~ C-Ya next month.

10 BILLION PESOS......

It's been an interesting month so far and it's not over yet. Tax time is always a wonderful time of the year for us all and this one has been a bit challenging for me and my accountants. I handed all my paperwork in and I thought everything was going along just fine when I got a call that the numbers seemed a bit over the top. This year I had to include the money I was spending in Mexico. The numbers are over the top, but you are looking at Pesos not American dollars. When you are looking at $16,500 Pesos it may look like you are in the money, but it's really $1,500 dollars. So needless to say it looked like I had about 2 to 3 million dollars to write off.....NOT! I couldn't figure out why they were having such a hard time, but I helped them figure it out. I think I told you that I bought a home down in Mexico and I had gotten the loan from a Mexican bank with GE as the lender. Well here we are with the communication breakdown once again. I really need to learn Spanish and so do we all if we are going to keep up with living in both countries. I send an e-mail down to Mexico asking the bank to send me my statements from Sept. to April for my loan payments. They can't find them and it takes a few weeks to get me in touch with the right person who might help me. Well they could help me, but when I phone them I ask for someone who speaks English to help me and they say they don't have anyone. What do I do now? I continue to e-mail until I find someone who I can communicate with. Finally I connect with someone who speaks a little English and I ask him if I can get my statements. He says yes and he e-mails me some statements and they are twice as much as the money as I was supposed to pay. My payment is around $950.00 American dollars and they have me paying about 2 times that amount. So now

I'm really freaked out and I start e-mailing every few hours to try to get this taken care of. I get nowhere fast...no one can help me. So I go to my bank and get all the statements from my account and guess what.....they have never taken any money from my account. OK now I am wondering....who's account are they taking it from? I call the guy who speaks just a little English and every time he tells me...Don't worry Mr. Miller we have everything in complete control....You are up to date on your account and your credit very great. Now I am really confused and I go back to my bank and to see if we can find anything....I'm thinking maybe someone is trying to make my house default, so they can take it back. Now I'm really not sleeping very well and starting to get very disturbed. I call the bank and ask where they are and they tell me in Mexico City and I really don't want to fly there. I ask the one person who is helping me...well kind of helping me...and I ask why are they taking out more money than they should and he replies back "I don't know, but it looks good for your credit" I ask...can you show me where is the extra money going and he says he will get back to me. This has been going on now for 3 weeks and yesterday we found where it was coming out of my bank each month just like he said. The only problem was the amount and the date when it was to be taken out was totally different than what we were told. So I call Mexico and both the bank and I are relieved that the money was coming out...but the amount is way out of line and almost double than I am suppose to be paying. He said that the extra money is going into an account. I tell him I don't want it going into an account and I don't want them taking any more than my payment. I ask him where can I get a statement of the extra money going into my savings? He says he is going to try to find it and find out why they are taking out so much. I don't know, but maybe if I knew Spanish things would be different....I don't think so.

IT'S CAMPER WORLD

Hey it's already July and I am freaking out about what to get Jane for Christmas. Yea.... You might think that I'm jumping the gun, but just close your eyes and think about last year and how fast it went. I guess you better start thinking about what you're going to get me. I think you could get me some 100 sun block for starters.......Boy am I dark and I'm starting to look a lot like an iguana...Just got back from Mexico and boy OH boy the humidity swooped in on the last couple of days I was there and it's kinda like breathing through a straw. The best thing during these times is a high-powered air conditioner and a pool. Let me tell you about the plane ride this trip. It seems as though no one can find a baby sitter anymore...the plane rides lately have half the plane filled with babies and toddlers maybe cause they ride for free, but man it's hard to get in a plane and know that for the next 3 to 4 hours it's going to be a cry and scream fest...not to mention the toddlers kicking the back of your seat for the entire time. The parents let it go as long as the kid is quiet....it gives them some relief......it kind of feels like a massage chair and all is fine until you try to sleep. Jane asked the folks behind us to try to get the kid not to kick her chair, but we think the parents were deaf, because the kid continued to kick the chair and scream the whole trip and all they did was smile. Maybe they weren't their kids.... maybe they were taking them down to Mexico to sell them and they were thinking about the big payday. Oh well....next time you fly bring the kids from the whole neighborhood....just call me and tell me where you're going. I told you we bought a home down in San Francisco Mexico last year and have been having a blast getting it ready for our friends and family and renters, well during this last trip something happened while I was there getting it ready for the next season of renters. I drove up to hang out in the pool for a while and noticed a small Toyota pickup parked directly across the street from my front door. About 10 feet away and the truck had a camper on the back of it and there were 4 or 5 guys standing around it talking. Now this was no ordinary camper...nooooooooooo this was a camper with some parts missing, like the cover to the electrical box and it was old and it was dirty and banged up and it looked horrible and they were talking about taking it off the truck and putting it up on palm tree trunks and bricks and sticks and.....OH my God what was happening right in front of my little casa. I asked them if they were going to put it right there and they spoke back to me in Spanish and ignored me. I went in my house and was freaking out....then I started to get real mad and then I went back out the front door and they were speaking English and I was blown away and there was a friend of mine (I thought) there helping them get it off the truck and he had some smart remark....like hey...we're going to get 4 or 5 of these and make a little camp ground out here....Real funny I thought, but I did laugh...only to think of how he would feel if this beautiful camper were in front of his new home. Boy did I have a couple of days of being real angry and thinking of how I could get them back for doing this to me....and then all of a sudden I remembered I was in Mexico not the U.S. and I started to chill.... And then after a few days I thought what the heck....who cares..... I came here to relax and I was bringing all my stress to my place of calm. So after a few days I chilled and it no longer mattered. This was a good thing for me to go through, because things are different in Mexico and I go there to wind down not up. So when I go back if there are 4 or 5 campers I will buy one and start the first KOA in Mexico which would be KOM....maybe I'm on to something. My computer crashed right after I watched a bootleg movie in Mexico... now I don't know if the movie had anything to do with the crash, but boy was this a coincidence. On one of the corners in our village they sell bootleg movies for a buck....while we were there Pirates of the Caribbean had just hit the movie theatres in the states and they had it for a buck and also the new Shrek movie was a buck. Just think of all the money we could save....they don't sell popcorn with the movies so you save even more. Just watch them on someone else's laptop, so you can do your work while you're there. Hey if all of this sounds like fun to you...give me a call and book a week this summer in our place we call Bungalow Bills. C-ya......Earl

IMPRESSING THE BOSS

It's August and I'm in a plane heading home from San Pancho Mexico and boy was this the trip of all trips. I traveled down to Mexico this time with my boss, Richard. A lot of you know him, but for those that don't this guy is the best boss anyone could have. This time of year is not the best time to travel down to Mexico unless you have come from the parts of the country that humidity is your favorite way to lose weight. I for one don't have the need for humidity for any reason at all. I believe the only good thing about it is you get to have fashion clothing changes about four times a day. Usually I have something to say about the plane ride, but this time it was real uneventful. We got to San Pancho and yes the camper was still right out my front door. I saw the guy who owned it and I noticed a for sale sign on it, so I asked him how much he wanted for it and I don't know if you remember what I said about it in my story, but this thing is a large piece of crap. I thought he would say something like 50 bucks and I will set it on fire…and to my surprise he said $500.00 and I almost laughed in his face. Then he said that it was a good thing for when his family visits, because it has two beds and it's very nice inside……………NOT……………I told him I didn't want to buy it, but I would pay him $200.00 to move it out from in front of my front door and our neighborhood. I know this guy doesn't have any money, but he just ignored me. Now I am thinking about burning it or having someone come by and running into it with a truck, but it would probably just sit there all burnt or wrecked and be one big mess. I thought for sure he would take the money, but he just avoided me while I was there. I knew it was going to be hot, but I really wasn't expecting the humidity to overtake my brain and body. I was so happy to get to my house, because I was going to run in and turn on my brand new air conditioning. I got to the house and I immediately turned on the air and guess what......it didn't work. You guessed it.......hot inside hot outside. A no win situation. I was so hot...I unpacked and went to take a shower and I had just bought a new awesome showerhead last time I was down here. I jumped into the shower and the front of the shower head fell on the floor at my feet. The water started to spray every direction except where it was supposed to go. I couldn't believe it and all I could say was...what's next.........the next morning we got up and Richard broke the coffee pot glass container. I tried to make some coffee into a bowl and the hot and I mean really hot coffee poured all over my hands. The shower was still usable it was just that the water went everywhere..got up the next morning the hot water heater broke and now we had no hot water......cold shower........ Up to this point everything was going wrong and the new day was about to begin...The day went on without a hitch and I thought everything from that point on was going to start going my way. As the evening approached the clouds started to turn black and when it started to rain I noticed the rain coming in under my front door...by the bucket full....the rug had to be taken outside and the thing was soaked and heavy. Awhile later the rain started to come down the beams in the house and it was raining in my living room. I'm not kidding. Now the rest of the rugs had to be taken out of the house. I went looking for someone the next day to fix my roof and he wanted $400.00 to fix it so I went to the bank to get the money. I gave it to him and that was the last time I saw him. In the morning I went to check on my email on my computer and guess what, no internet connection. I was out of my mind at this time and I was just waiting for the next disaster. The next day I heard from a friend of mine, Faurest, who had just purchased a brand new Land Rover with all the bells and whistles. I'm told that it cost around $130,000 and it was so beautiful.....well we wanted to go looking at some real estate so he came by and we hopped in and went to see property. We came to a rather large puddle that was actually a street flooded with water and I said let's not go through it and he said no problem....

this is a brand new Rover that lifts up 12 inches with a push of a button. I hadn't told him what had happened to me up until that moment, because I didn't want to jinx anything. We started going through the water and all of a sudden the water was coming up over the hood and halfway up the windows and the Rover stalled and the water started filling up the floors and coming in the doors and it was getting deep quick.... the beautiful white leather seats were getting soaked with muddy water and I could no longer see my legs. We knew we couldn't do anything and we couldn't open the doors so we just sat there. The car filled up with muddy water and a bunch of guys showed up to push us out, but they couldn't so they went and got a truck and hooked up the bumpers and pulled us out of the water. My friend just laughed and said.....what else could we do?..............nothing, but I'm sure glad it wasn't my car. About an hour later he picked us up in another brand new Land Rover and we went looking at more property. We waited five days for the guy with the Freon to show up and we left without ever seeing him. We did go buy two fans that helped us go to sleep. My boss found a new coffee maker in a village and I do believe it was the only one in town. All in all it was a disaster trip, but it was really fun. I don't think my boss is planning on buying any land, but I do think I could talk him into another vacation. Anyone want to go on vacation with me next month?

COULD I DIE?

This is the end of August and I'm still waiting for a real hot summer. I'm heading down to Mexico at the end of the week and I know it is going to be hot down there. As a matter of fact, it will be somewhere in the 90's and the humidity will be around the same. It makes it hard to breathe sometimes....no not really it's just kind of like breathing through a straw. And that's not so bad if you have a real big straw. So I hope you all got to read the last months story about my spelling and my punctuation. It's true I can't spell and my punctuation is usually..............it makes it a lot easier. I got quite a lot of mail and it was all positive and that made me really happy. Last month's story was supposed to be about my hip surgery, but I wanted to keep it a secret. I know a lot of you know I have needed a new hip for a couple of years now. Most of you who know me or who see me walking or should I say limping down Main Street, know when you see me that it is almost over for my hip. I have been waiting until I can't stand the pain anymore and it has been getting almost unbearable. I just haven't wanted to go into surgery, because I don't have the time to recover by sitting around. I also have been a little scared about the surgery. OK maybe a whole lot scared. Over the last six months I have done everything I could to stall the surgery and I couldn't figure it out until about three weeks ago. I was really scared I wouldn't make it through the operation....yea I thought I might not wake up after the surgery. I hadn't been telling anyone, but I guess a lot of people were feeling my apprehension, because when I told people I wasn't getting the surgery...they were also relieved............and a lot of them said they could feel that I wasn't ready. First off let's get to the doctor's office where they told me to exercise at least 3 days a week for the past 3 months and during that time I got to the gym twice. They also told me that the surgery would go a lot better if I was to lose about 20 pounds. Well I was eating like there might not be a tomorrow and the more I thought about it the more I ate and over the course of the last two months I gained about 14 pounds. I would look at cookies or anything bad for me and say to myself....if I am going to die I will never have those again and I would eat a bunch of what ever I thought I would never get to have again. Pizza and cheeseburgers were full on and usually I stay away from them just to stay healthy. I was trying to come up with any reason I could not to get the surgery on the date they had set for me. I don't know if you are like me or maybe I'm a freak, but when I feel that something might go wrong with something I'm doing I think about it and evaluate it to go with my gut feeling. For about three months I was feeling like something might go wrong and I kept trying to make it work in my head, but it kept coming up wrong. Then the day came when I had to go to the doctor's office to do my pre op stuff. I was really scared about the whole thing and I told the doctor that I was real uneasy about the operation and the doctor really made me think about it more. The doc told me that there was a chance that my sciatic nerve might be cut and I would end up with drop foot for life. That made me really weird and then the doc said that about 1 to 3 % of the people who get the operation get it infected and have to have the hip taken out and they have to go back to the hospital for a few months to heal. At this point I have pretty much made up my mind to not go through with it until I can no longer walk. I'm totally freaked out and I just want to run out of the hospital screaming. I leave the hospital and tell the doc I'll see them on Thursday and I really was thinking I probably would go through with it. The next day a friend calls me and tells me that Pete Wilson is taking calls on his radio station at KGO and he is a bit paranoid about his hip surgery that is coming up the next day is asking people to call in and let him know about their hip surgery stories.. I tried to make a call, but got too busy, but I did want to call and tell him I was feeling the same way he was. Well I didn't get to talk to him and the next day I hear that he died of a heart attack while getting his hip done. I didn't know the man, but I felt like he was family. When that happened I said that's it...not me.........I called and canceled my surgery and I'm glad I did. I really felt like I wasn't going to make it just like Pete. For now I am setting up a lot of appointments that will help me clear for the right day. I will let you know! If you see me limping down Main Street honk and wave and yell out "He's alive! He's alive!"

LOVE CHILD

This is February while I am writing this.... about a week after Valentine's day. I hope you had a great day....**I love the Love Day....**One more reason to love my wife....and just one more day to let her know how much I really love her. I wanted to get her something really nice that we both could enjoy, so I ordered a nice night shirt on line from a company I saw over and over on the TV. They also had a package that came with it full of fun stuff. If you saw the commercial you probably bought something too. They made it very sexy and very fun,,, and I wanted what they were doing in my life. I know that I should have thought way ahead, and went to the mall and taken things into my own hands...So Valentine's Day I was pretty excited about the mail coming but about mid-day I was getting kind of worried. So I called the company and all the phone lines were busy and the email line was not working. So as it started to get dark and the evening was setting in I called and I found out that the pj's were going to be delivered by UPS, so I relaxed a bit knowing that the trucks were probably filled with gifts for men and women everywhere and probably a lot of pajamas.... and until everything is delivered they will keep working, but I really started to get worried because it was starting to get darker and darker. I called the hot line and finally got a hold of someone. We went through all the credit card stuff and the address stuff and he tells me that I never made an order. OK now I'm not feeling the love at all, so I tell him everything I went through and he tells me he's sorry......I tell him..... sorry.....I had a real romantic evening planned tonight and how was I going to tell my wife that we were going to have to go to bed naked? I asked him....would you like to tell my wife why she is going to bed naked tonight? I was pretty mad, but really felt bad about not getting a present ahead of time and depending on the on-line stuff. So a little later that evening I tell my wife about the fact that nothing is coming and she say's OH that's Ok just having you is enough for me….."How sweet it is" so when it was time for bed we had no pajamas and I was bummed and I could see so was she, so I told her I wouldn't wear my flannels and we just went to bed. I want to thank the pajama company for messing up. **I love the Love Day.**

IS THAT YOU STANLEY?

Hey it's May, but if you are reading this it's June, but really it's May. It's the week that was so hot I thought I was in Mexico without the humidity. Wow it really was hot.....and I liked it. I heard a lot of people complaining about the heat. Usually I am complaining about the cold, but there were a few moments this last week I caught myself complaining to myself about the heat. When I would hear someone else complain I would pipe up and say something stupid like.....it's really not hot enough for me....and smile and laugh. What a real pain in the butt I am.... if you can't hang with the heat I totally understand. I was over in Walnut Creek today and it was 101 and I don't mean the highway I mean one hundred and one degrees.... Hot hot hot hot......I caught myself not digging it at all, as a matter of fact I couldn't stand it and it made me feel sorry for the NO HEAT people.

I went to a Stanley Cup hockey game with a friend and he had been asking me to a few games and our schedule always made it impossible to go. I got pretty excited about the game, because I had never been to a hockey game before....as a matter of fact I always thought of the hockey game as a pretty violent game. When we got there everybody was in purple and I mean everybody...I'm not sure, but I think I saw Barney. Then it struck me I really don't like going to games that much and my friend reminded me of a time he had given me tickets to a 49er game and it was the hottest day in history in the stadium and I swore off going to games....any kind of games....as we headed towards our seats I could only think of how comfortable we would be for the next three hours and then we got to the seats. Now I remember why I don't like being a rather large man…the seats were made for children and small girls. As I wend my way down to my seat past a few happy spectators they had to stand because there wasn't any room between their legs and the seats. When I sat down my knees were tight up against the seat in front of me and also touching the guys back in front of me. I had bought a coke and when I went to put it down I found two cup holders right by my legs and I couldn't figure out which cup holder was mine. I put it down on the side with the small girl next to me (she was about nine and the seat seemed a bit snug for her), but at least I could see it when I needed a drink….and the guy on the other side of me didn't think I was rubbing his leg every few minutes when I did go to get a drink. Now I remember my friend talking about the article I wrote about the last time he gave me tickets…. he said it was funny, but as I write this story I have a feeling after he reads this one he probably won't take me to a game or give me tickets ever again. The weirdest thing about the hockey game was that I really enjoyed it…..I totally loved it. I loved the violence….I mean I really loved the violence……the guys were slamming each other into the wall and slugging each other in the head every chance they could….I kind of wanted to suit up and whack a few guys myself…I loved the really bad Mexican salad….I loved the seat that was half the size of my butt….I loved the fact that the guy in front of me kept his arm around his girlfriend the whole game and so I had to keep my leg tucked up under my seat…I loved the game so much I might become a purple shirt dude and throw out all my Hawaiian shirts. I really….I mean really loved it…….I caught myself doing the shark mouth thing with my hands…..you pretend you are the shark with your arms closing like a shark bite……now if most of you know me…you know I wouldn't do that for anything…. but I got all caught up in the hype…The music was right up my alley also….AC/DC…which is one of my favorite bands…seems as though they get quite a lot of air time at the games at full blast. It's like going to a game and you get the concert for free. The fans are wild and now I understand why…..this game rocks. I looked at my ticket and saw that it was over one hundred dollars to see that game and if you would have asked me before the game I would have told you that you were crazy out of you mind to pay that much to see a game....but I would say.....what a bargain....at this point.....now if any of you have extra tickets next season and want to take me.....I'll go and I'll buy you a hot dog or some peanuts..Thanks Mike!!!

SUDDEN DEATH

Areal crazy thing happened a couple of weeks ago and I thought I would share it...of course I am.....that's why I write....OK..a couple of years ago I got invited to go see Billy Joel and Elton John together....I don't know if you remember the story, but I got to sit in the front row.....what a show....thanks Kenny. My buddy Phil called and asked if we wanted to go see. Billy Joel and at first I thought maybe I would pass, because I have so much going on and I sometimes need to say no. So I said yes...of course...and got myself all wound up by listening to my IPod all day with Billy songs. We headed over to the Arco arena in Sacramento and when we got there I noticed something....everyone was about my age and in the parking lot it looked like we were all headed to an AARP convention. When Billy came out on stage he made a comment and said...Billy couldn't be here tonight I'm his father.....Billy is home combing his hair....It struck me that the thousands of folks were all over 50 and came to rock out. As I sat there I started to think about the new 50 being 40...you've heard that....well when it comes to music, because we are from the 60's..... 50 is the new 25, cause......WE ROCK!...So everyone pretty much knows the words to every song...and then the ultimate song comes on....you got it the PIANO MAN....the stadium becomes one big sing along.....enough so that Billy doesn't have to even sing and he lets the audience take over.....Whenever I go to a concert...I have a select number of friends that when a big hit starts to be played I take out my cell phone and call a friend. So as the evening was going on I called different people for different songs. When the Piano Man came on I called Richard a friend in Benicia and dialed his number and held my phone up in the air and let the song ride its way through

the air waves right into his ears..…..I never say "hey listen to this", because it is too loud and I just assume they will figure it out. I held the phone up pretty much for the whole song and when it was over I flipped it shut.…..I was leaving the concert and I looked at my phone messages and this one person I let hear the Piano Man was on my list of missed calls about 5 times in the last half hour…I called him and he answered.…..in a panic…are you all right? and where are you? I said hey dude…I'm at a Billy Joel concert…and he said after swearing at me for a minute.…..you jerk.…….when I got the phone call I thought you phoned me and when it connected..…..
I thought you had a heart attack and fell on the ground somewhere where there was music playing, because it went on and on.……I thought you were laying somewhere dying.….So I called the Benicia police and had them head over to your house.……yup three squad cars and a bunch of police trying to get into my house to find me dead on the floor listening to music full blast. He told me they went around the house looking in all the windows and became worried and decided to get a ladder and look in the bedroom windows. He also told me that when they couldn't find me they thought I might be somewhere else and were going to be checking around town. ..He also told me that the one thing the police did notice when they were checking to see if I was dead in my car…was that my registration was expired..…..Nice police work.…..I guess my friend thinks that 50 is the new 80..…..for me anyway..…..I was touched by his concern.. next time I will call out my name during the song. Now I know what my friends think about my age and I still will go rock out and even at the age of 70 I will be the new 30. Old rockers never die..….. and neither do their mullets..…..ETM

WHICH WAY TODAY DAD?

I am sitting in an airport in Manchester New Hampshire and it's 4:30 in the morning.......what the heck am I doing up this early? I just flew out to visit my dad who is 83 and in a nursing care home. He is doing great as far as what an 83 year old can do. He doesn't hear so well, doesn't walk well at all, doesn't remember much, talks about moving to a condo on the beach soon, say's maybe we should get his car ready for him to drive for when his legs get better, but all in all he's doing great. I noticed he was kinda sweet on an 85 year old woman at the home and I really think he has sparked up a real relationship. We were going by her room....I was walking my dad in his wheelchair and as we rolled by he said that's my girlfriend.....right in front of her...and from her wheelchair she smiled and held out her hand for me. Boy this was so nice to see....I think we all need love and I guess it doesn't matter how old we get. It really put a smile on my face to see my dad light up whenever we would pass by her room. I had dinner with them at the home and I tell you.....If they don't die from natural causes....they could die from boredom of the food.....usually I will eat anything, but when the meal came...I had to pass.....a lot of peas and carrots....and a lot of mushy stuff..... the best part of the dinner was the tapioca pudding....I did eat that....A couple days ago my dad asked me if we could go visit a friend of his and I said yes...and so we left the home and drove off towards Boston and he was giving me directions....my first mistake...no map...no address...no city where we were headed...no clue....we drove on and on and on and every now and then he would say...this looks familiar turn right.....so we would turn and turn and turn and turn....well we drove around from town to town....very scenic. Lots of pretty trees....about 3 hours later I decided to tell him maybe we could go looking tomorrow......he said OK and I actually think he forgot what we were doing anyway...so we went back to the home. I picked him up the next morning and he said hey do you want to go see my friend...and I said sure.....so when we were leaving the home he said go that way....totally the opposite direction from the day before. We drove up towards Maine and after about an hour I pulled over and got a map.....landmarks weren't happening anymore, he was really lost...I think I found the town where the person lived and I thought we were set.....my dad said hey that's her street and so I drove down it and I said which house is hers? and he said I don't know I have never been here before. I asked how are we going to find her? and he said...we will just look for her car...and I said great what kind of car is it? and he said it's black....I should have known....well we drove up and down the streets looking for a black car and..... nope....no black car...no friend...no WAY....then he said she told him to meet her at a restaurant at 1:00 and I said what restaurant and he looked at me like I was supposed to know....the look was precious. He said well there aren't that many restaurants up this main road....why don't we just go into all the parking lots and see if I can find her car. I didn't want to tell him, but there were about 25 restaurants along this highway, because it was a tourist area and it was Friday the beginning of Memorial day weekend and there were thousands of cars in every parking lot....we pulled into a few and then finally we pulled over and went into a restaurant and had lunch...he said maybe she's in here...NOPE...we headed back to the home and I went back to the hotel to rest......over the 2 days looking for someone he wouldn't tell me who we were looking for I bet we drove at least 5 hours and a couple hundred miles.....silly me......my dad has dementia and I guess I am in denial.....I went to pick him up later and he never mentioned the person again. Just to be able to spend the time hanging out with him was worth a million dollars....and about a million for gas....I'm not sure I really want to get older at this point....I think this weekend really made me think about who I am and what I am doing at this time in my

life....I think the key is exercise and I really don't get that much....
I am going home today with a whole new attitude....I need to make
some changes and I better make them fast...or I will be looking for
my dad's friend soon...Oh let's talk about the airport security for a
moment....My new hip has posed quite a big hassle at the airport
check-in...I BEEP every time I go through and I'm getting tired
of it...everywhere I go I get to get the full treatment for being a
terrorist. I know I don't look like a terrorist...do I? Each time I go
to the airport I get to go through the box and get searched by very
special folks...sometimes I get new employees and they take quite a
bit of time and really make me feel like I've done something wrong
by beeping....some don't talk and aren't nice to me and I think some
really want me to have a bomb and to be a terrorist, so they can
arrest me and be in the news....I guess I should make the best of
it...it's to keep us all alive and free.

YOU WANT TO PUT THAT WHERE?

Hey something weird happened to me just before I left to Mexico last month. I went to the hospital to get my blood checked just as a regular routine and the day after I went in I got a call from the urology department and they wanted me to call them. I called and talked to a lady who was very helpful as usual, but when I asked what was up she told me that they would like to see me...now...and I asked what for and she said that my PSA numbers were way off. I asked what that was and she said she wasn't that sure, but it had something to do with my colon. I set up an appointment for the next day and had a pretty hard time sleeping. I thought about what it could be and I took it to the furthest point I could, because that's what I do. Went to the hospital the next day and felt pretty good and checked in and went in the room and the doctor came in and we talked and he told me that my PSA numbers were out of line and they were concerned that it could be cancer. I was relieved to find out that it was my prostate they were talking about. He went over all the things that I would be going through and if it was cancer what kind of treatments were available. He made me feel real good about the chances of dying, as he told me that if it was cancer I wouldn't die from it. That made me feel ok, but then I had to think about the treatments and the biopsy and just the fact that where things are suppose to come out....things were going to be going in. Then I wasn't so happy and he scheduled an appointment...and I took off to Mexico for five days to mellow out. In my head I was not having a problem at all with what the outcome would be...the way I live..... every day is a gift and I live everyday as if it were the only one I get. Most folks think I'm a little crazy, but I gotta tell you.....I'm a lot crazy......So I get back and go to my appointment to do the biopsy and I gotta tell you I was scared. I went into the room and the big needles and the tools they were going to use on me were on the little cart next to the bed...this is the first time I ever had to put my feet up in the stirrups....I have heard a lot about women having to do it, but I never really paid that much attention to it until it was my turn. I was ok with the doctor being in the room, but then a nurse came into the room and I felt a little uneasy. Naked with just a little bit of the little tiny night shirt they have you wear. Legs spread and in the stirrups and exposed to the world....I thought I was going to pass out. I have always loved it when a doctor says.... this is going to hurt just a little.... how does he know?....has he had this done to him lately? I don't think so, and I have always wanted to do to them...what they are doing to me and tell them this is going to hurt just a little. Well it did hurt just a little, but the whole experience was embarrassing to say the least. I would go into it, but I don't want to scare anyone out of going to have it done, because it is so necessary. I will continue to get checked every six months from now on. I got to let you know that a few days before I went in for the biopsy I went to see and be a part of a spiritual healer that came to town. Now I know some of you might think that I might be a little off, but my thought is **BRING IT ON!** I believe that everything is possible with great faith and the power of positive thinking. When I called to get the results for the biopsy the doctor told me that there wasn't any cancer and I knew that before he talked to me, but I wanted to be sure. Our health is the most important thing we have.....if you are reading this story and you haven't had a check up lately.....**get your Butt to the doctor.** Life is great and with all the medical stuff that has happened to me I need to let you know again.......

EVERY DAY IS A GIFT.

MELLOW YELLOW

Life has been pretty stressful around my life lately. So I thought I would take off and go to Mexico. I know you think I am always going away, but really I'm not. You probably think I go down there for vacation...not always. This trip is mostly business and I do mean business. I am going to let you all in on a little secret....I am writing a book and I really need quiet time. It's hard enough just to think on a minute to minute basis......let alone when I am all stressed out. So I got on a plane and brought my laptop...... I am actually writing this story in our little casa late at night. Just jumped in the pool to wake up and here I sit pounding away at the keys trying to make my deadline. I really am trying to simplify my life so as not to be so stressed. The first thing I did was to buy the new book that Oprah has been pod casting around the world. Awakening to Your Life's Purpose is the name of it and I'm into it a few chapters. You know, I already feel a little more mellow and am getting mellower as the days go by. I have been involved in quite a few "getting in touch with myself" programs over the last 35 years and I feel pretty in touch. With what I am not sure of, but I am a creature of habit and I will always go for the next thing that comes along that might help. There was the Guru period, EST, the whole hippie movement with all the peace and love, and tons of programs over the last bunch of years and lately the Secret and Be Here Now stuff. I am the light, I am the light, I am the light.....although I am not much brighter, but I am the light. I hope when my book gets done you all will buy it and then I can go on Oprah and tell what I think is my story......Not like the guy that wrote 1,000,000 Little Pieces.....boy did he have a hard time with everyone on the planet for awhile. Even Oprah made him come back on and tell everyone in the world that he had lied. I am going to make it real clear and right up front I am going to call my book **My Life as I Remember It…..Not Necessarily the Truth**. This way no one can call me a liar or even dispute what I have to write about, because I am taking it from my memory……even my first story begins when I was eight and that was 50 years ago. How much stuff do you remember from 50 years ago? Now you understand the title of the book. I do not want to be on Oprah asking everyone to forgive me, because I got the story a little out of whack. Sometimes when I am writing I think to myself……did that really happen or did I just make that up over the years. I can tell you one thing for sure……I am not a liar….Sounds like Nixon doesn't it? How about Clinton….. I did not have sexual relations with that woman. Now we know those guys were lying and they didn't have to go on Oprah and tell the truth. I'm telling you right up front, my book is about what I think I remember. NO LIES….just 50 years of what I think might bring a smile to the faces of those who read it. I am asking all of you to help me out….. and if any of you know Oprah or know someone who knows her…..or even her friend Gail……help me out and tell them that I am writing a book and you know it's going to be good and Oprah should put it on her book club….books to read. You know every book she tells people to read becomes a best seller. The only reason I just bought the New Earth book I am reading today is because Oprah said to read it. I bought the Secret because of Oprah and I also bought the cd's and I thought I already knew the secret. So let's start sending happy thoughts towards Oprah and with all the self help people she knows…..she will probably pick up the vibe without ever really knowing where it came from….and when my book is done she will probably just call me and let me jump on her couch like Tom Cruise did. You know just sitting here talking about it gets me all revved up and ready to put on a lot of camera makeup and start rolling.

THE END

Is this really the end?
I hope it's not the end. I feel it's just the beginning of a
friendship that is going to last a lifetime. Thank you for
reading all the crazy stories that happen to me month after
month after month after month.

Thank you Jeff Dennis, Donna Rowles and Richard
Freedman. Yea it's done...Or is that Yeah it's finally done?

A New Beginning
*I couldn't leave you without giving you a couple of
my favorite recipes from the last 30 years.*
Cookin' With Earl

The Crackies win the "Best of the Year" 2002 Award!!

"CRACKIES"—It's Hershey Time

40 Saltine Crackers…Yes I said Saltine Crackers
(Just for fun…try a corner of the pan with graham crackers) Jane
says don't..I say do!!
1 cup of brown sugar—1 cup of chopped walnuts
2 sticks of real butter—6 or 7 Hershey bars

Grease cookie sheet…lay crackers in a single layer all across the cookie sheet so you cant see the bottom any more. Melt butter in a saucepan—add sugar. Boil for 3 minutes—pour over crackers—spread evenly with a spoon or brush. Bake @ 350 for 12 minutes. Take out of oven and lay Hershey bars all over the top of the crackers. While hot and melted spread evenly—sprinkle nuts all over the chocolate. Now put in the refrigerator. When ready…take out and break yourself off a piece and you will understand why it takes the C.W.E. Award for 2002….Easy to make and great to eat!

ALOHA FROM THE GAZEBO IN NAPILI

This recipe was stolen from Jerry & Lucy Corson the owners of the very famous Gazebo Restaurant in Napili, Maui.

Macadamia Nut-Sauce Pancakes

Ingredients: 1—10 oz package of dream whip topping mix
18 oz ice cubes and water
4 oz butterscotch topping (cold)
8 oz maple syrup (cold)
Mac-Nuts in pieces

Preparation: Fill a 5 qt. stainless steel mixing bowl with ice, add water to brim. Let stand for a few minutes to allow bowl to get very cold. Temperature of ingredients is very important. Pour water and ice from mixing bowl into a large bowl. Quickly add to mixing bowl in the following order. Water, syrup, butterscotch topping, and dream whip mix, quickly get the mixing bowl to the mixer and bring the mixer to maximum speed as soon as possible without making a huge mess! Mix for approximately 10 minutes. Time may vary with mixer and temperatures. Sauce should be very thing and stay on a spoon when turned upside down. Sauce is topped on the pancakes and Mac-nuts are spread over the sauce.

The story as it goes!! I brought you this recipe in October of 1998 and I am here to tell ya….I believe everyone on the planet read it because whenever you go to the Gazebo now you will have to wait in line, but it is so worth it….or just follow the recipe and invite some friends with hula skirts over and chow down. The owner was so nice to share this with all of us. The Gazebo has been serving up pancakes for the past 28 years and the only thing that hasn't gotten bigger is the restaurant. Now it's not such the well kept secret it once was. Folks like Dustin Hoffman, Troy Aikman and a whole bunch of other stars make this one destination they won't miss while on vacation. I would like to give you directions, but I would rather you take me…so call me and I will pack and we will have a blast! If you are going to make these at home call me and I'll drop by for breakfast!. Mahalo…C-Ya

Made in the USA
San Bernardino, CA
21 January 2015